The Indo-European Dialects

ALABAMA LINGUISTIC & PHILOLOGICAL SERIES NO. 15

Antoine Meillet

The Indo-European Dialects

Translated by Samuel N. Rosenberg

UNIVERSITY OF ALABAMA PRESS
University, Alabama

Contents

Translator's Note

IN PREPARING THIS EARLY WORK OF ANTOINE Meillet for readers of English, I have permitted myself to take at face value the author's own statement on the occasion of its reprinting in 1922: "A work such as this, with its brief presentation of just a few ideas, does not lend itself to revision or enlargement". The present volume is, then, neither more nor less than a translation of the French text of 1908, together with the author's prefatory remarks of 1922. Of the latter, only the first half, or those observations having a general interest, are presented here under the heading "Author's Foreword to the Second Printing". The others, related to particular chapters, are given in the body of the text (or in notes), with each insertion marked *(Add.)*. Indices, lacking in the editions of 1908 and 1922, have been added for the convenience of the reader.

As far as possible, and within the bounds of reason, I have used only linguistic terminology current during the first decade or so of this century. This limitation was dictated not only by the statement quoted above, not only by a distaste for chronological incongruity, but also and much more importantly—since terminological change implies conceptual change—by the desire to avoid the danger of distorting Meillet's ideas and attributing to the author concepts and distinctions that were not part of his linguistic construct. Thus, sounds are "sounds" and not, variously, "phones" or "allophones" or "phonemes". So, too, the reader will find no attempt in these pages to distinguish several meanings of *l'indo-européen commun* or to render the term with any modifier other than "Common": to reject either the comprehensiveness of the term or the idea of *communauté*, which it so clearly expresses, would have been to destroy a controlling principle of the original work.

In the transcription of examples I have followed the same conventions as the author. Should these require any elucidation—the transliteration of Sanskrit, for example, or the orthography of Lithuanian, or the use of spaced roman letters instead of italics for many Osco-Umbrian words—the reader is referred to the section "Transcriptions" in any edition of Meillet's *Introduction à l'étude comparative des langues indo-européennes* [No. 3 in the Alabama Linguistic & Philological Series]. All French glosses have, of course, been translated into English; Latin and other glosses, generally given for a very specific purpose, have been retained and are usually accompanied by English translations.

To Professor Frank Banta of Indiana University I wish to express my deepest thanks for his very generous and helpful counsel.

S. N. ROSENBERG

Bloomington, Indiana
April, 1967

Abbreviations

Aeol.	Aeolic	Goth.	Gothic
Alb.	Albanian	Gr.	Greek
Arm.	Armenian	Hind.	Hindi
AS.	Anglo-Saxon	Hom.	Homeric
Att.	Attic	Ice.	Icelandic
Av.	Avestan	IE.	Indo-European
Balt.	Baltic	II.	Indo-Iranian
Boeot.	Boeotian	Ion.	Ionic
Bret.	Breton	Ir.	Irish
Bryth.	Brythonic	Iran.	Iranian
Celt.	Celtic	It.	Italic
Cret.	Cretan	Itn.	Italian
Cz.	Czech	Lat.	Latin
Dor.	Doric	Lesb.	Lesbian
E.	English	Lett.	Lettish
Fal.	Faliscan	Lith.	Lithuanian
Fr.	French	Locr.	Locrian
G.	German	Osc.	Oscan
Gaul.	Gaulish	Oss.	Ossetic
GAv.	Gatha Avestan	Pahl.	Pahlavi
Germ.	Germanic	Pers.	Persian

Pol.	Polish	Umbr.	Umbrian
Pruss.	Prussian	Ved.	Vedic
Russ.	Russian	Wel.	Welsh
Sax.	Saxon		
Serb.	Serbian	H	High
Skr.	Sanskrit	L	Low
Sl.	Slavic	M	Middle
Slov.	Slovak	Mod	Modern
Sogd.	Sogdian	O	Old

BSL   *Bulletin de la Société de linguistique de Paris*
IF   *Indogermanische Forschungen*
KZ   *Zeitschrift für vergleichende Sprachforschung auf dem*
        Gebiete der indogermanischen Sprachen
MSL   *Mémoires de la Société de linguistique de Paris*
Voc.   Old Prussian Vocabulary of Elbing

Author's Foreword
to the Second Printing

TO JUDGE BY OUR OBSERVATIONS OF ALL THE ancient Indo-European peoples — the Celts no less than the "Aryans" of India and Iran, the Germanic tribes and the Greeks, the Slavs as well as the Italic peoples — the elements that in prehistoric time composed the Indo-European "nation" were loosely bound together and did not constitute a stable political unit. A leader like the legendary leader of the Bituriges, Ambigatos, could found a great Celtic empire, but such an empire could no more survive its founder than the empire of Alexander. Indo-European unity was national rather than political. And there is no reason to believe that any part of the "nation" had a lasting, dominant influence over the other parts. Thus isoglosses must have crossed in all directions throughout the Indo-European area, and we have no grounds for expecting to find bundles of isoglosses that are either coincidental or

simply near one another—such as those, for example,
between southern France, which is relatively close to Latin,
and northern France, which is quite aberrant with respect
to Latin.

Unfortunately, it is difficult to form a valid picture of
all the ancient Indo-European dialects. For the western-
most group, represented by Germanic and Italo-Celtic, we
do not have truly archaic texts. If we had, for this group,
an equivalent of the Indo-Iranian Vedas or Gathas, or an
equivalent of the Homeric texts, Indo-European dialectology would have a degree of precision that it now
lacks, and the comparative grammar of the Indo-European
languages would present a quite different appearance.

It is noteworthy, for example, that stems such as *dō-/*dǝ-
or *dhē- (*dhō-)/*dhǝ-, from athematic roots with "perfective" meaning, provide Italo-Celtic, Germanic, and no
doubt Armenian with presents of perfective aspect, such
as Lat. *dat, volt* (cf. Ved. aorist *avr̥ta*), OHG. *tuot-,* and
provide Greek and Indo-Iranian with aorists, such as Skr.
ádāt, ádhāt, Gr. ἔδομεν, ἔθεμεν (see Meillet, *BSL,* XXIII, 70).
But all we have is a glimpse of this. We must at least add
this isogloss to those already known and point out, in this
regard, that Slavic and no doubt Armenian occupy a
position midway between the Latin and German type on
the one hand and the Greek and Indo-Iranian type on
the other.

For lack of sufficiently ancient data covering the bulk
of the territory of Indo-European, we invest Common
Indo-European with a form as close as possible to that of
Greek and Indo-Iranian. This is somewhat illusory. The
discovery of Tokharian has shown, for example, that verb
endings in -*r* were not peculiar to Italo-Celtic; however,
these endings are hard to place in the system as con-
structed according to Greek and Indo-Iranian. Masculine

nominatives without endings, e.g., OLat. *quo-i,* Osc. p u - i, Umbr. *po-i,* are surely very ancient. Subjunctive types in -*ā-,* e.g., OIr. *bia* in contrast to *benaim* or OLat. *ad-venat* in contrast to *ven-iō,* cannot be the result of new developments in Italo-Celtic; the phenomenon appears to be fundamentally Indo-European.

To form a valid picture of Common Indo-European, it would surely be necessary to correct further the image provided by Greek and Indo-Iranian, and to have wide recourse to non-innovational data supplied by Germanic and Italo-Celtic.

The Germanic, Celtic, and Italic idioms present, indeed, certain common innovational tendencies.

To be sure, the special pronunciation of initial syllables found in Germanic, Gaelic, and Italic is not found in the Brythonic group of Celtic. To be sure, the relatively long quantity that has been attributed, no doubt correctly, to Latin initial syllables, and that should probably be attributed to Italic in general, is not the same thing as the strong initial stress observed in Gaelic and Germanic. It is nevertheless striking that in all three groups the initial syllable tends to undergo special treatment in the word. This unique initial situation is manifested, particularly in Latin, in the closing of medial short vowels and, in Osco-Umbrian, in the occurrence of syncope. In any case, initial syllables are in a category by themselves. As a result, final syllables tend to weaken considerably—another feature common to Germanic, Celtic, and Italic.

Still another striking feature is the tendency to vocalize, as it were, intervocalic consonants. This innovation varies in its realization from one language to another. In Celtic, it appears with particular importance: Brythonic, in which initial *y* and *w* become voiced consonants, voices intervocalic voiceless stops, whereas Gaelic, in which *y* and *w*

become voiceless consonants, changes intervocalic voiceless stops to voiceless spirants. In Germanic, voicing of
intervocalic consonants affects only the spirants; moreover,
it is often checked by special circumstances: Verner's law
in Common Germanic (affecting the spirant closing the
initial syllable of a word), or the Wrede–Thurneysen law
(certain in Gothic[1] and to be assumed elsewhere, as in Old
Saxon, which contrasts *tehando* and *tegotho* 'tenth'). In
Common Italic, only the sibilant -*s*- is voiced; voicing of the
original voiceless spirants in the types Lat. *medius, animāli-
bus, figūra* (cf. Osc. m e f i a í, l u i s a r i f s, f e í h ú s s) is
peculiar to Latin. However, this tendency to weaken intervocalic consonants stands in curious contrast to the stability of intervocalic consonants that characterizes Greek,
Baltic, and Slavic.

Vowels, especially short vowels, are subject to environ-
mental influence in Germanic, Celtic, and Italic. The
phenomenon, known as *umlaut,* dominates vocalic development in West Germanic, North Germanic, and Gaelic.
Latin shows a contrast between *volo, volens* and *velim, velle;*
and a preceding guttural is enough to prevent the shift
from *e* to *o* in *gelu, gelāre,* for example. This vocalic depen-
dency contrasts with the characteristic stability and independence of vowels in Common Greek, Baltic, and
Slavic.

In the realm of morphology, Germanic, Celtic, and Italic
all give the expression of verb tense a degree of importance
that this notion did not have in Indo-European. The contrast between present and past was expressed unclearly and
inconsistently in Indo-European, by means of the primary
and secondary endings and, in one dialect group, by means
of a subsidiary word, the augment (see below, chap. XIV).
By different processes, Germanic, Celtic, and Italic came
to express the preterite by means of stems proper to the

preterite. And, unlike any of the other Indo-European languages, these developed preterites for the "subjunctive". Thereupon, the secondary endings could serve a present function: Lat. *fātu-r* is a present, whereas Hom. *φάτο* is a preterite (see Meillet, *BSL*, XXIII). In Irish, *-beir*, corresponding to Ved. *bhárat*, and *berat*, corresponding to Ved. *bháran*, are presents, as are *berid* and *berit*, which correspond to Skr. *bhárati*, *bháranti*.

There are grounds for supposing that Germanic, Celtic, and Italic underwent similar influences. After the Italo-Celtic period, Italic ceased undergoing these influences and underwent others. On the contrary, Germanic and Celtic, remaining in adjacent regions, developed in part along parallel lines. They both developed a clear stress accent that in Gaelic, as in Germanic, was placed on the initial syllable. The stops developed similarly: voiceless stops came to be aspirated, and voiced stops tended to unvoice to some extent; things did not go so far in Celtic as in Germanic, where a complete shift occurred, but the point of departure was the same for the two languages.

There are, then, various types of relations to be observed among the Indo-European languages. It is often difficult to trace them to their historical circumstances.

It is important, in any case, to distinguish between areas of common phonological and grammatical systems and areas of common vocabulary. Common vocabulary indicates above all common civilization and is, therefore, of particular interest in the study of history.

Concordances of juridical and religious vocabulary in Indo-Iranian and in Italo-Celtic, revealed by J. Vendryes (*MSL*, XX, 265), are to be explained as a feature of social structure common to the peoples of the two groups. They do not imply any dialectal relationship.

What makes the comparative grammar of the Indo-European languages possible is that there was once a certain Indo-European "nation" and that each of the groups into which that nation divided became a nation in its turn—an "Aryan" (Indo-Iranian) nation, an Hellenic nation, an Italo-Celtic nation, etc. In each region, a governing aristocracy succeeded no less in imposing a single language than in establishing its own type of social structure.

Characterizing each of these groups are not only the innovations they produced when undergoing common development, but also new common tendencies reflecting the initial unity of the group—tendencies that remained operative after the rupture of that unity.

For example, Indo-Iranian had preserved the type **bharā,* corresponding to Gr. φέρω, Lat. *ferō,* OIr. *-biur,* Goth. *baira,* in the 1st-person singular primary active. Gatha Avestan remained faithful to this type. But there was a tendency to add *-mi,* and we find the addition already crystallized in the earliest Vedic texts, in the later sections of the Avesta, and in the Persian Achaemenian inscriptions. If the Gathas were not extant, we should no doubt believe the type Ved. *bhárāmi* to be Indo-Iranian. It is possible that the process began as early as the Indo-Iranian period. But it was not generalized until Indic and Iranian began to develop separately, and many Iranian forms would be unintelligible if we had to admit *bhárāmi* as the Common Indo-Iranian type (see Meillet, *MSL,* XXII, 220). The almost complete identity of morphological structure in the two languages led naturally to identical innovations.

The continuing action of new common tendencies is an even stronger proof of the kinship of dialects than the preservation of innovations already realized during a period of common development.

Author's Prefatory Note

THIS BRIEF WORK STEMS FROM A COURSE GIVEN at the Collège de France in 1906–1907. In it I have attempted to bring into focus the much debated question of the Indo-European dialects. To treat thoroughly each of the subjects that a complete examination of the problem would involve, I should have had to review the entire comparative grammar of the Indo-European languages. Instead, I have limited myself to mentioning only briefly the facts already known, usually without even referring to the works in which they are studied.

The table of contents provides a sufficient indication of the subjects treated; I have not seen any need to add an index.

I thank Mr. Maurice Grammont and Mr. Joseph Vendryes for their kind aid and valuable advice.

The Indo-European Dialects

Introduction

NOWHERE IS COMPLETE LINGUISTIC UNITY TO be found. An individual speaks in perceptibly different ways, depending on his physical and mental state at a given moment, on the persons to whom he is speaking, and on place, time, and external circumstances.

Nevertheless, the inhabitants of a single locality tend to speak in the same way, insofar as differences of social status are not manifested in differences of speech, and insofar as certain groups of individuals do not mark their independence through recourse to linguistic peculiarities. This unity is not tangible anywhere; its existence is purely abstract until it has been formulated and fixed by grammarians; it is the norm to which everyone tends to conform; when any individual deviates from it, the other native inhabitants of the locality are aware of the deviation. It is true that no one quite realizes the norm; the locality can, besides, understand strangers whose speech is somewhat different. They can, particularly, understand

persons of different ages and, indeed, observation shows
that successive generations bring changes of varying
importance to the speech of a locality.[1] Apart, then, from
differences attributable to special circumstances or to the
age of individual speakers, there is in every locality a
certain ideal linguistic type, of which all actual realizations
are only approximations. Since individual variations are
of no basic interest, it is the ideal type—itself varying,
however, with successive generations—that must be the
main object of linguistic study. Deviations are important
only insofar as they may serve to account for previous
development and to indicate and explain future changes.

The evidence afforded by literary languages has encountered considerable disdain; it nevertheless continues
to be used. This evidence has, among its shortcomings,
that of concealing many individual peculiarities and that of
allowing most changes to appear only after their completion—which is to say that their origins remain hidden. It
does, however, have the merit of immediately revealing,
not individual and momentary accidents, but a norm; for a
written language is fixed and generally reproduces the
ideal type to which all speakers attempt to conform.
Having approached written languages first, linguistics has
quite appropriately been concerned with the essential
features of languages and their general type. This circumstance, though often deplored and though still having
certain infelicitous effects, was in reality highly favorable to
the development of linguistics at the time of its origins.

Let us look now at a single language, spoken over an
extensive area that includes a considerable number of
separate localities; apart from the changes resulting from
word-borrowing or imitational phonetic and grammatical
substitutions, the changes brought about by the natural
succession of generations are realized independently in
each locality. Since these changes proceed from general

causes, they take place for the most part in a more or less large number of centers, ordinarily grouped together. Since, on the other hand, change is produced independently in each locality, each of the various isoglosses marking the boundaries of innovations on a linguistic map is autonomous and independent of the others. Strictly speaking, then, in the ideal case here considered, there exist only boundaries of separate linguistic events; there are no dialect boundaries, for the lines of the various phenomena intersect and never coincide except by accident. A. Dauzat has collected a number of statements by eminent Romance scholars (H. Schuchardt, G. Paris, P. Meyer) who have formulated this principle in the clearest and most decisive terms.[2] The principle has been confirmed elsewhere — wherever, as in the area of Lithuanian, matters have been examined closely. C. D. Buck (in *Classical Philology,* II, 243) has recently shown, with a great mass of evidence, that the Greek dialects likewise reveal independent isoglosses.

Nevertheless, linguistic changes do influence one another. Moreover, the group of localities where a given change of some importance takes place is a group subject to the action of common causes. Thus it is possible for the boundaries enclosing the groups of localities in which several independent innovations take place to coincide completely, or at least to approach one another and often run almost parallel. A group of localities in which a series of concordant changes is thus independently produced, which are consequently enclosed together by a certain number of isoglosses, and which contrast in this respect with adjacent areas, constitutes a *natural dialect.*

The notion of a natural dialect is not, then, as rigorous as the notion of isoglosses delimiting a group of localities with respect to a particular phenomenon; the dialect is not delimited by one line but by a series of lines distinct from

one another. Though somewhat fluid, the notion is nevertheless a real one, and the inhabitants of certain regions
have the impression of speaking a dialect that distinguishes
them from the inhabitants of one or another adjacent
region.

The developments described in this brief theoretical
sketch have often been realized; the evolution of the
Romance languages provides fine examples. Nowhere
better than in France, for example, can we observe the
autonomy of isoglosses and their partial parallelism, which
together characterize natural dialects clearly perceptible
to their speakers.

The existence of natural dialects so defined in no way
undermines the independence of local speech. With time,
local idioms grow increasingly apart, and the natural result
of this divergence would be the ultimate appearance of as
many distinct languages as there are localities in the area
originally occupied by a single language. The French *patois,*
which show remarkable differences and are often mutually
unintelligible even at a distance of a few dozen kilometers,
give us an idea of the end toward which this evolution
moves.

But the evolution does not reach its goal. Before it can
succeed in denying language its natural concern, which is
communication among the greatest possible number of
people, it is interrupted by the extension of some common
language, i.e., a generalized local idiom such as French,
which is essentially the idiom of Paris, or a mixture of
idioms such as English, which combines elements borrowed
from several different sources. First, the common language
is superimposed on local languages; then, being more
useful and meeting the needs of the speakers better, it
eliminates them completely. Historical circumstances, such
as conquest, political unification, etc., initiate these extensions, whose subsequent development is motivated by the

advantage that the inhabitants find in speaking a language of the broadest possible use. Conversely, every political division, every interruption of economic and social relations, gives rise anew to linguistic differentiation. The history of languages is thus composed of a succession of great unifications and great differentiations — to which we must add the partial unifications that are constantly taking place in areas of varying size, even within the most differentiated groups of idioms, and the differentiations that occur in even the most unified groups of idioms.

This kind of development has occurred twice so far in the history of the Italic languages. What at a given moment was clearly a single language broke first into two groups: Latin and Osco-Umbrian. These then underwent differentiation, and Oscan, Umbrian, and Latin came to constitute three distinct languages, none of which, in historical times, was intelligible to a speaker of either of the others. The local idioms were then differentiated in their turn; the inhabitants of the area just outside Rome spoke differently from those within the city; for example, what was *lūna* in Rome was *lōsna* in Præneste. Political circumstances, by giving Rome political supremacy, brought about the extension of the Roman dialect, which, though heavily influenced by this assimilative process and taking on a number of extramural peculiarities, absorbed the other Latin dialects and eliminated not only Oscan and Umbrian, but also the other languages spoken in Italy, viz., Etruscan, Gaulish, Venetic, Messapic, Greek, etc. The dislocation of the Roman empire brought with it the dislocation of the linguistic unity thus created; once again, as many distinct dialects developed as there were localities or, at least, small feudal groupings. Later, the rise of national consciousness led each nationality to adopt a single language as a national means of communication; this language has ever since tended toward the elimination of local or regional idioms.

The development is quite advanced in France, where the substitution of standard French for the *patois* is largely an accomplished fact in most regions.

Such are, in brief outline, the general principles of the evolution of natural dialects. We are purposely leaving aside the two types of dialectal unity that are achieved through generalization: (1) unity resulting from the extension of a given type of idiom through conquests (e.g., the Doric idioms of Greece) — a kind of unity that does not stem from autonomous innovations having approximately the same boundaries but from an initial sameness that is then generalized; (2) unity resulting from imitation of the idiom of a dominant group. These two types of unity through generalization are often distinguishable only theoretically from the unity of natural dialects.

It remains for us to apply these principles to Common Indo-European. Here there are several phases to distinguish.

By the time of its initial attestation in literary or epigraphic texts, each one of the Indo-European languages had already passed through a period of individual unity, following the period of general Indo-European unity. Extant languages do not allow us a direct return to Indo-European; between Attic and Indo-European, for example, there was a Common Hellenic period. The linguistic state of none of these common periods is attested directly; we can form an idea of them only through correspondences among languages that are known through written texts. Thus, Common Greek is the system of correspondences among the Hellenic dialects: Ionic and Attic, the Aeolian group (Lesbian, Thessalian, and Boeotian), the Arcadian and Cypriote group, the Doric idioms, etc.

Indo-European is likewise nothing but the system of correspondences among the common languages so defined: Common Greek, Common Germanic, Common Slavic, Indo-Iranian, etc.

It is not, then, a matter of applying the above principles of dialectal development to a language, but rather to one of various systems of linguistic correspondences. The problem thus takes on a very special appearance.

The language whose existence is supposed by the correspondence–system known as Indo-European must have been spoken over an extensive area comprising a certain, probably sizable, number of distinct groups of inhabitants. It was then possible for changes to occur that covered only part of the area; if we could observe Indo-European directly, we should find isoglosses there. These lines express partial groupings within systems of correspondences: instead of finding that each of the groups attested follows its own path of development, we observe that some languages fall into a single type when contrasted with others. For example, Indo-Iranian, Baltic and Slavic, Albanian, and Armenian all show affricates or sibilants in positions where the other Indo-European languages have gutturals: Sanskrit has *ç*, Avestan *s*, Slavic *s*, Lithuanian *sz* (i.e., *š*), Albanian *s*, and Armenian *s*, where Greek has *κ*, Latin *c*, Celtic *k*, and Germanic *x* (whence *h* and *g*, *γ*, as the case may be). The study of the Indo-European dialects is an examination of these groupings of linguistic correspondences and an attempt to determine whether they derive from dialect groupings of the Indo-European period.[3]

The distinction between Indo-European dialectal phenomena and innovations occurring in each language after its separation from the central group cannot be made clearly. Both cases involve, by definition, phenomena realized independently — and subsequently showing the same features — in languages of like structure, such as the various languages of the family indeed were at the time of their separation. Long after the separation, there were still similar innovations taking place in languages that were already quite well differentiated. The *e* of Lat. *tepidum* became *ie* in some of the Romance languages, as in Itn. *tiepido,* Fr. *tiède;* similarly, the *e* of Common Slavic **teplŭ* in one of the Slavic languages: Pol. *ciepły.*[4]

Lacking any decisive criterion, we can only assemble all of the ancient phenomena that meet certain defined conditions; their scope is found in the extent to which they meet these conditions as a set.

First, the linguistic events considered must occur not only in the oldest languages attested, but also in the common languages as we know them through comparison of attested languages: we can use only phenomena of Common Greek, Common Slavic, Common Germanic, etc. (the languages known in German as *Urgriechisch, Urslavisch,* etc.). Moreover, these phenomena must not appear in the common languages as recent innovations due to causes peculiar to those languages.

Secondly, the phenomena must have a certain oneness that would presuppose the action of identical causes operating in a given region, and that would eliminate the possibility of an independent development arising sometime after separation. All details easily explained by universal tendencies of human speech must be rejected.

Lastly, the common phenomena must be found in languages that have been neighboring languages; there must be no crossing of regions. Establishment of the continuous dialect areas of Indo-European is facilitated by our observation that the separation of the Indo-European languages does not seem to have brought about any dislocations: one of the main conclusions of the present study will be that the area occupied by the Indo-European family has been widened without any essential change in the respective positions of the dialects.

Before entering into a detailed study of individual phenomena, we have two questions to discuss, viz., the relative
importance of lexical data, and the existence of dialect
groupings postdating the separation of the Indo-European
languages.

By themselves, instances of lexical concordance, or cognate words, are very important, as J. Gilliéron points out in
the case of French dialects in the studies based on his *Atlas
linguistique*. But it is hard to see their usefulness in Indo-
European dialectology. On the one hand, the number of
Indo-European etymologies is small and cannot be compared with the number of Romance etymologies. On the
other hand, the words given as cognate are words of
general meaning and, to the very limited extent to which
they are special or somewhat technical terms, we do not
have any way of determining precisely to what degree the
instances of concordance stem from cultural phenomena:
if a given term is wanting in a group of dialects, it may be
because historical circumstances or technological changes
brought about its disappearance; and if some other term is
found only in certain other dialects, we may suspect a
borrowing attributable to commercial influence. We need
first to determine whether there is any glimpse of such
phenomena.

As for dialect groupings postdating the separation,
there is another possibility to be considered. The peoples
that carried Indo-European across Europe and a part of
Asia, and that developed each of the attested language-
families, did not necessarily separate immediately into the
population groups that are known to have existed at the
beginning of historical times. Certain groups may have
split off only after a period of common development when
the common form of the historically attested group became
fixed. Various facts lead us to posit an Indo-Iranian period
antedating the Indic period and the Common Iranian

period, as well as an Italo-Celtic period followed by an
Italic period (prior to the Osco-Umbrian stage on the one
hand and the Latin stage on the other; it goes without
saying that the "Italic" period may have antedated the
entry of Indo-European tribes into Italy and may thus
have had no connection with the Italian peninsula); there
may also have been a Balto-Slavic period.

The peoples comprising these linguistic groups, which
were later divided, must have consisted from the outset
of individuals belonging to different localities. The momentary stage of common development through which
they passed was no more sufficient to bring about complete linguistic identification than sufficient to eliminate
all tribal, phratral, or other distinctions. Within these
groups, then, we may find traces of Indo-European dialectal distinctions. Further on in the present work we shall
be led to posit certain isoglosses between Iranian and Sanskrit and between Celtic and Italic.

This intermediate stage of common development shows
up in coincidences of detail, in unique innovations, in
forms that reproduce neither an Indo-European function
nor even a general Indo-European type—in a word, in all
peculiarities that two languages cannot introduce independently and that presuppose prolonged and close relations,
precisely those relations which may be imagined among
the groups of colonists and conquerors that propagated
each of the Indo-European language-families.

We shall be led, then, to determine the basis for
positing the most firmly established groups, viz., Indo-
Iranian, Italo-Celtic, and Balto-Slavic. Only after this
study of post-separational phenomena will it be possible
to survey the dialectal phenomena preceding the separation, i.e., those of Indo-European time proper.

The developments just outlined constitute only a few of
the many very complex events that were brought about by

the spread of the Indo-European languages. There is no doubt, for example, that territories first settled by a certain tribe speaking a certain dialect could have been, and often were, settled at a later time by another tribe speaking a different dialect; various indications still point to such series of substitutions in a few parts of Greece.[5] It would no doubt be difficult to recognize phenomena of this type in the prehistoric development of the oldest languages of the Indo-European family. If that aim is ever to be achieved, however, we must first establish the Indo-European dialects with a certain precision.

When we have succeeded in determining to some extent the dialectal phenomena of Indo-European time, we will have one of the most necessary bases for the study of each of the common languages — Indo-Iranian, Common Greek, Common Slavic, etc. First, we will have an initial relative chronology of events, since we will be able to distinguish between Indo-European phenomena and those of subsequent date. Secondly, we will know from what particular form of Indo-European each language arose and how its ultimate development was conditioned by that form. Lastly, and perhaps most importantly, we will be able to distinguish between Indo-European phenomena and those resulting from conditions peculiar to each of the groups that carried the language into new territory — conditions such as the degree of unity of the group spreading Indo-European, the size of the group, the reaction of peoples speaking other languages, the gradual scattering of Indo-European speakers over an increasingly vast area and their gradual loss of contact with one another, etc.

If the actual object of the present study is the investigation of phenomena of Indo-European time, common to this or that part of the area of Indo-European, the main result will be to reveal the extent of originality in the development of the great families of languages; simple comparison will show which innovations belong to them individually. Almost all current handbooks, at least apparently, treat without distinction phenomena that are of different dates and types; in grouping dialectal phenomena for the most part already known, we shall try to demonstrate the possibility of discerning successive phases in the development of the Indo-European languages between the period of unity and that of the oldest written texts.

chapter one

Vocabulary of the Northwest

A. FICK, IN HIS ETYMOLOGICAL DICTIONARY,[1] set up an Indo-Iranian vocabulary and a vocabulary of the European languages in contrast with each other. This procedure seemed valid as long as scholars accepted the idea that European was characterized by a certain number of phonological and morphological innovations produced after the separation of the two groups. Today, however, no one believes in those peculiarly European innovations. The fact that Indo-Iranian lacks some words that are well attested in most of the languages of Europe has nothing characteristic about it, nor does it argue the early separation of the Indo-Iranian group. There is no Indo-European language that does not lack certain words which are present in most of the others; for example, the Indo-European nouns for 'son' and 'daughter' (Skr. *sūnúḥ* and *duhitā́*) are wanting in Italic and Celtic, and yet there are no words more commonly attested over the Indo-European area in general.

It is true that some of the terms which Indo-Iranian

lacks refer to important agricultural notions, e.g., 'plough' (Lat. *arāre*), 'grind' (Lat. *molere*), or to related notions, e.g., 'salt' (Lat. *sāl*), but it is easy to see how the speakers who carried Indo-Iranian across Asia might have lost a few terms relating to agriculture, and all the cogency of the observation has disappeared with the recent discovery of an Indo-Iranian name for a cereal (Skr. *yávaḥ*, Av. *yava-*) and a formation from a root meaning 'grind' (Pers. *ārd*, Hind. *āṭā* 'flour'). Agriculture was being practiced at the time when Indo-Iranian was separated, and the question of a peculiarly European vocabulary is now an idle one.

There is, however, a quite large group of words that appear in the dialects of the North and West (Slavic, Baltic, Germanic, Celtic, and Italic), but are not found in the others (Indo-Iranian, Armenian, and Greek). Many of these words have a cultural reference, and their occurrence in the dialects of the North and West would indicate a cultural development peculiar to the peoples who spread those dialects. Examples follow.

AGRICULTURAL TERMS:
'Sow': OSl. *sěti*, Lith. *séti*, Goth. *saian*, Lat. *serere* (*sēvī*); OSl. *sěmę* 'seed', Lith. *sémenys*, OHG. *sāmo*, Lat. *sēmen*, OIr. *sīl*, Wel. *hād* (cf. Lat. *satus*). Greek ἵημι 'I send' is not a cognate; it has long been recognized that ἵημι, ἧκα is to Lat. *iaciō*, *iēcī* as τίθημι, ἔθηκα is to *faciō, fēcī*. Sanskrit *strī* 'woman' has no relevance here; to say that the 'woman' was called the 'sower' because, at a certain stage of cultural development, women cultivated the land, is simply a witticism; besides, we should expect **sātrī* or, at most, **sitrī*. Only Arm. *hund* 'seed', possibly formed like *serund* 'descendants' (cf. *serel* 'beget'), could perhaps be related to **sē-* in the languages of the Northwest; but the root is apparently not represented elsewhere in Armenian, and it is known that *h* derived from IE. **s* is not ordinarily preserved in that language.

The connection is therefore highly suspect, and the existence of *sē-* 'sow' is certain only in the Northwestern group.

'Grain': Lat. *grānum*, Ir. *grān*, Wel. *grawn* (plur.), Goth. *kaurn*, OSl. *zrŭno* (Serb. *zȑno*); Lith. *žìrnis* 'pea'. It is not at all certain that Skr. *jīrṇáḥ* 'aged', etc., is a cognate; even if it is, the fact remains that the meaning 'grain' is limited to the languages of the Northwest, and so definite a peculiarity of meaning is sufficient to characterize a group.

A word denoting a cereal-derived food: Lat. *far (farris)* and *farīna*, Umbr. *farsio* f a s i u 'spelt-cakes, (Lat.) farrea', OIce. *barr* 'cereals', Goth. *barizeins* 'made of barley', OSl. *brašĭno* 'food', Serb. *brȁšno* 'flour', Russ. *bórošno* 'rye flour'. There is no reason to see Skr. *bhárvati* 'he chews' as a cognate, nor, consequently, Av. *-baourva-*.

'Furrow': Lat. *līra* (and *dē-līrus*, *dēlīrō*, *dēlērō*), OHG. *(wagan-)leisa*, MHG. *leis* 'wheel track', OSl. *lěxa* 'garden plot, πρασιά'* (Russ. *lexá*, Serb. *lijèha*, Cz. *lícha*, no doubt an oxytone originally); Lith. *lýsė* 'farming square or strip'.

'Apple': OSl. *ablŭko* (Russ. *jábloko*, Pol. *jabłko*), Lith. *óbŭlas*, Lett. *ābols*, OPruss. *woble*, OHG. *apful*, OE. *æppel*, OIr. *aball*, MWel. *aual*. The city-name *malifera Abella* in Campania provides a trace of the existence of the word in Italic, but the introduction of a Mediterranean type with its Doric name μᾶλον, whence Lat. *mālum* (or Common Greek μῆλον, whence Itn. *melo*), brought about the disappearance of the old word in Italy.

'Pig': Lat. *porcus*, Umbr. *porca*, p u r k a (fem. acc. pl.), OIr. *orc*, OHG. *farah*, OE. *fearh*, Lith. *par̃szas*, OSl. *prasę* (Russ. *porosjá*, Serb. *prȁse*, Pol. *prosię*). The alleged Gr. πόρκος, of which Varro speaks, is not found in any Greek text and is no doubt only a word borrowed from an Italic language by the Greeks of Italy or Sicily. The Northwestern word *pork₁os designates only the domestic pig, while the Common Indo-European word *sū-* (Lat. *sūs*, etc.) denotes both domestic and wild swine.

'Bean': Lat. *faba,* OPruss. *babo,* OSl. *bobŭ;* relation to the Germanic word, OIce. *baun,* OE. *bēan,* OHG. *bōna,* has not been established. Albanian *baθє* is quite distant in form.

'Mildew': Lat. *muscus,* OHG. *mos,* Lith. *musaĩ,* OSl. *mŭxŭ.*

'Dig': Lat. *fodiō,* Wel. *bedd* 'pit', Lith. *bedù* 'I dig' and *badaũ* 'I prick', Lett. *bedre* 'pit', OSl. *bodą* 'I prick', perhaps Goth. *badi* 'bed' (originally 'dug in the earth'? – see R. Meringer, *IF,* XIX, 488). The initial *β* suffices to make us reject Gr. *βόθρος, βόθυνος.*

'Rye' (of which there seems to be no Neolithic evidence) has a designation which does not extend beyond Slavic, Baltic, and Germanic: OSl. *rŭžĭ,* Lith. *rugỹs,* OPruss. *rugis,* OIce. *rygr,* OE. *ryge,* OHG. *rokko.* There is a word for 'oats' which cannot be reconstructed with certainty, but which is obviously common to Slavic (*ovĭsŭ*), Baltic (Lith. *aviżà,* Lett. *auzas,* OPruss. *wyse*), and Latin (*avēna*).

NAMES OF BIRDS AND INSECTS:

'Thrush': Lat. *turdus,* OIce. *þrǫstr,* Lith. *strãzdas,* OSl. *drozdŭ* (with assimilation of the initial consonant), and *drozgŭ.* Greek *στροῦθος* cannot be considered a cognate because of the *ου,* but also because of the *θ,* which corresponds neither to Germanic *t* nor to Latin *d;* there would be a *b* after the *r* if it were a matter of **dh.*

'Wasp': Lat. *vespa,* OBret. *guohi,* OHG. *wafsa,* Lith. *vapsà,* OSl. *osa.* Baluchi *gvabz* 'bee, wasp' must be rejected because of its isolation in Indo-Iranian; the voiced element *bz,* moreover, presents a certain difficulty; comparison with the root **webh-* 'weave' explains nothing, for it is hard to see how the meaning of that root could be related to 'wasp'.

'Hornet': Lat. *crābrō,* Wel. *creyryn,* OHG. *hornuz,* Lith. *szirszũ* (accus. *szìrszenį*), OSl. *srŭšenĭ* (Serb. *sȑšljēn*).

The word **nizdo-* with the special meaning of 'nest' in: Lat. *nīdus,* OIr. *net,* OHG. *nest,* and, with some changes,

Lith. *lízdas* and OSl. *gnězdo*. On the contrary, Arm. *nist* means only 'seat' and serves as verbal noun for the primary verb *nstim* 'I am seated' (aorist *nstay*), and Skr. *nīḍáḥ* has kept the meaning of 'seat, place where one is settled' alongside that of 'nest'.

NAMES OF TREES:
'Alder': Lat. *alnus*, OHG. *elira*, Lith. *elksnis*, OSl. *jelixa*.
'Elm': Lat. *ulmus*, Ir. *lem*, OIce. *álmr*, Sl. **jilĭmŭ* and *jilĭma*.
'Yew': Ir. *eo*, Wel. *yw*, OIce. *ýr*, OE. *īw* and *eōw*, OHG. *īwa*, Lith. *ĕvá*, OSl. *jiva*.

TECHNICAL TERMS:
'Strike' (esp. in smithery): Lat. *cūdō* and *incūs* (*incūdis*), Ir. *cuad* and *coach*,[2] OHG. *houwan*, Lith. *káuju*, *káuti* 'beat, strike, fight', *kúgis* 'hammer', *kovà* 'fight', OSl. *kujǫ* 'I forge', *kyjĭ* 'hammer'.

'Cut': Lat. *secō*, OSl. *sĕkǫ;* Lat. *secūris*, OSl. *sekyra* 'axe'; OHG. *seh* 'knife', *sega* 'saw', *sahs* 'knife'.[3]

'Plait, braid': Lat. *plectō*, OHG. *flehtan*, and OSl. *pletǫ* represent a single form, rather different from Gr. πλέκω and the Sanskrit noun *praçnaḥ* 'braided object'. The treatment of **-kt-* found in OSl. *pletǫ* is normal before a postpalatal vowel. (OSl. *nošti* is a classic example of the outcome of **-kt-* before a prepalatal vowel.)

'Wheel': Lat. *rota*, Ir. *roth*, Wel. *rhōd*, OHG. *rad*, Lith. *rātas*. The corresponding word in Indo-Iranian (Skr. *ráthaḥ*, Av. *raθō*) means 'chariot'.

'Pole (of a vehicle)': Lat. *tēmō*, OHG. *dīhsala*, OE. *þixl*, OIce. *þísl*, OPruss. *teansis*.

'Shield': Lat. *scūtum*, Ir. *scīath*, OPruss. *staitan* (*scaitan?*), OSl. *štitŭ*. If Lith. *skýdas* and Gr. ἀσπίς (ἀσπίδος) are related, they differ at least in having a *d* where the other languages have a *t*.

'Handle': Lat. *ansa*, Lith. *ǫsà*, OIce. *œs* 'hole (for a lace)'.

WORDS OF SOCIAL RELATIONS:

'People': Osc. *touto*, Umbr. *totam* (accus.), OIr. *tūath*, Goth. *þiuda*, Lith. *tauta*.

'Stranger, guest': Lat. *hostis*, Goth. *gasts*, OSl. *gostĭ.* While Gr. ξένϝος is related, it has an entirely different form.

'Debt': OSl. *dlŭgŭ* (Serb. *dûg*), Goth. *dulgs*, OIr. *dliged* (*dligim* 'I owe'). The root diphthong of Slavic having circumflex intonation, the Slavic word is no doubt borrowed from Germanic; there is no positive reason to believe that the Germanic word is a borrowing from Celtic.

'Pledge': Lat. *vas* (*vadis*), Goth. *wadi*, OIce. *veð*, OHG. *wetti;* Lith. *vadŭti* 'redeem, release'.

'Dominate': OSl. *vladǫ*, Lith. *valdaũ* and -*veldu*, Goth. *waldan*. Cf. Ir. *flaith* 'sovereignty' (certain Scandinavian forms also have a *t*) and Lat. *valeō*.

MISCELLANEOUS:

'Man', designated by the expression 'earthly': Lat. *homō*, Goth. *guma*, Lith. *žmũ* (*žmónės*).In Indo-Iranian, Armenian, and Greek, on the other hand, man is called 'mortal': Hom. βροτός, Arm. *mard*, Av. *marəta* and *mašyō*, OPers. *martiya*, Skr. *mártyaḥ, mártaḥ*.

'Beard': Lat. *barba*, OHG. *bart*, Lith. *barzdà*, OSl. *brada*, whence the adjectives Lat. *barbātus*, Lith. *barzdótas*, OSl. *bradatŭ*.

'Polished, smooth': Lat. *glaber*, OE. *glæd*, OHG. *glat*, Lith. *glodùs*, OSl. *gladŭkŭ*.

'Ice, coldness': Lat. *gelu* and *glaciēs*, OHG. *kalt* and *kuoli*, Lith. *gélmenis* 'bitter cold', OSl. *golotĭ* 'ice' and *žlědica* 'ice, frost'. Γελανδρόν ψυχρόν occurs in Hesychius, but this gloss is related to Sicilian γέλα, which must be a borrowing from Italic. The Sicilian dialects seem to have been a little less resistant to borrowings than the other Greek dialects; see above, πόρκος; W. Schulze (*KZ*, XXXIII, 223) has recognized in λίτρα another Sicilian borrowing. Compare, too, Lat. *calēre* with Lith. *szìlti* 'become warm'.

'Word': Lat. *verbum*, Goth. *waurd*, OPruss. *wirds*, Lith. *var̃das*. The root is Common Indo-European.[4]

'Push': Lat. *trūdō*, Goth. *þriutan*, OSl. *trudŭ*.

'North wind': Lat. *caurus*, Goth. *skūra-*, OHG. *skūr*, Lith. *sziáurè* 'north, north wind', OSl. *sěverŭ* 'north'.

'True': Lat. *vērus*, OIr. *fīr*, OHG. *wār;* OSl. *věra* 'faith'.

'Abundant': Ir. *menicc*, Goth. *manags*, OSl. *mŭnogŭ*.

'Sea': Lat. *mare*, Ir. *muir*, Gaul. *(are-)morica*, Goth. *marei* and *mari(-saiws)*, Lith. *mãrès*, OSl. *morje*. This noun for 'sea' is common only in the languages of the Northwest; it seems, nevertheless, that Sanskrit has a trace of it in the obscure word *maryádā*.

On the other hand, the prohibitive negation **mē* is attested only in Indo-Iranian (*mā́*), Greek (μή), and Armenian (*mi*); elsewhere it is totally lacking. Independent disappearance in Slavic, Baltic, Germanic, Celtic, and Italic is hardly likely; in the languages which once had **mē*, forms of the word are still used today, and there is no difference, in this respect, between the ancient and modern stages of Greek, Armenian, or Persian. However, the phenomenon is too isolated to prove much.

One or another of these cognate groupings may be fortuitous, and nothing special may be affirmed concerning any one of them. Taken in general, however, they cannot be fortuitous at all, especially in view of the categories of meaning into which they fall. There is, then, a certain amount of common vocabulary in the languages of the North and West, and this common vocabulary appears to stem from a common cultural development.

chapter two

Indo-Iranian

OF ALL THE GROUPS OF DIALECTS BASED ON A
period of common development postdating the Indo-
European period, Indo-Iranian is the only group attested
by direct evidence.

The evidence is the name by which both the Indic and
the Iranian peoples designated themselves. Avestan *airya-*
(opposed to *tūirya-* and *anairya-*), OPers. *ariya-* in *Dārayavāuš
ariyačiθra* 'Darius of Aryan family': this noun was known to
the Greeks (῎Αριοι) and the Armenians (*Arikh*), and is
extant today; *Ērān* (now pronounced *īrān*), the modern
name for the land of the western *Aryas,* represents a genitive plural *aryānām*. Sanskrit *ā́r(i)yaḥ* designates the
speakers of Vedic; *árya-,* too, is possible; the word *ā́r(i)yaḥ*
is the same as the Iranian word, except for the length of
the vowel (vṛddhi).

The etymology of the noun is unknown. One might see a
connection with Skr. *áryaḥ* 'favorable', but this seems
tenuous and of little interest.[1] There is no justification for

adducing Arm. *ari* 'brave', which is surely not to be isolated from *aru* 'male' and *ayr* 'man, (Lat.) vir'. As for a connection with Ir. *aire* (gen. *airech*), gloss to *primas,* it is clearly wrong; Ir. *aire* cannot be separated from Ir. *ar* 'before' (cf. Ir. *airchinnech* 'first, chief, [Lat.] princeps', Wel. *arbennig*); it is a word of the same family as Gr.πέρι, πρό, etc. and Lat. *prīmus,* etc. The **aryo-* on which Ir. *aire* is based is also found in Gaul. *Ario(-manus),* a compound whose first term has nothing to do with the proper noun **Arya-* denoting the people who spoke Indo-Iranian.

*Arya- is a proper noun whose meaning is irrelevant here, but whose existence is evidence of the original unity of an Indo-Iranian people that was fragmented only later.

From this well-established case, we may infer the type of phenomena by which to recognize such common development postdating separation from the rest of the Indo-European family: Indo-Iranian presents a whole series of special features that are found nowhere else and that stem from the period of common evolution peculiar to the group. Following are some of the features that cannot be fortuitous:

(1) The mid vowels, *e* and *o,* which without exception remained distinct in all the other Indo-European languages, combined with *a.* Leading to the loss of morphological gradations marked by *e* and *o,* this fusion profoundly changed the entire flectional system; the result was the emergence of quantitative gradations of the type $\breve{a}/\bar{a}$. This situation is eminently characteristic of Indo-Iranian.

(2) Indo-European **ə,* instead of combining with **a* as it does everywhere else (except to some extent in Greek, where, however, it never gives ι), becomes *i.* Before and after *y,* however, **ə* gives *a,* even in Indo-Iranian.

(3) Clusters of the type voiced aspirated stop+voiceless

stop become voiced stop+voiced aspirated stop (Bartholo-
mae's law), e.g., *-bh* + *t-* gives *-bdh-*, *-bh* + *s-* gives *-bzh-*, etc.
The other languages all show a development in keeping
with the ordinary rules of Indo-European, i.e., voiced
aspirated stops, like those not aspirated, unvoice before a
voiceless element. The occasional traces of a development
such as that defined by Bartholomae's law, which have
been pointed out in other languages, are all either false
or uncertain. It is true that *-θσκ-* gives *-σχ-* in Greek
(πάσχω from *παθσκω), but that is a special case and can
hardly be made the basis of a general law. Greek ἔσχατος
has been explained by *eghs-qo-*, but nothing proves that ἐξ
is based on *eghs;* the Locrian form ἐχθός and the forms
analogous to it represent the normal development of *-χθ-*
from *-kst-* in Greek, and ἐκτός owes its *τ* to an analogy
with ἐντός; if ἔσχατος is to be derived from ἐξ (and this is
not at all clear), it is enough to posit *eks-ko-* giving *ἔσχο-*.
As for αἶσχος and Goth. *aiwiski*, if they are cognates, that
may be shown either by *aikʷhskos* giving αἶσχος (type
πάσχω), or quite simply by *aikʷskos* giving αἶσχος (type
ἔσχατος). Greek, then, offers no trace of Bartholomae's
law, and neither do the other languages.

(4) All stems ending in a vowel (*-a, -ā, -i, -u*) form their
genitive plural in *-n-ām*. Such infixing of *-n-* is not found
elsewhere except in certain Germanic dialects, and then
only with certain types of stems.

(5) Stems in *-ā-* have, together with endings in *-ā-*,
endings of the genitive–ablative type Skr. *-āyāḥ*, OPers.
-āyā, and Av. *-ayå*. In Armenian and Celtic we find a trace
of *-(i)y-* in certain cases of *-ā–*stems, but nowhere do we find
the type *-āyā-*.

(6) Third-person imperatives have a final *-u*, e.g., Skr.
bháratu, Av. *baratu*, OPers. *baratuv*.

(7) The parallelism of certain flections is absolute, as
in the 1st-person personal pronoun:

	Skr.	Av.	OPers.
SINGULAR			
Nominative	*ahám*	*azəm*	*adam*
Tonic acc.	*mā́m*	*mąm*	*mām*
Atonic acc.	*mā*	*mā*	
Aton. gen.-dat.	*me*	*me*	*maiy*
Tonic gen.	*máma*	*mana*	*manā*
Tonic dat.	*máhya(m)*	(GAv.) *maibyā*	
Ablative	*mát*	*maṯ*	*ma*
PLURAL			
Nominative	*vayám*	*vaēm* (i.e. *vayim*)	*vayam*
Aton. acc.-gen.-dat.	*naḥ*	*nō*	
Tonic acc.	*asmā́n*	*ahma*	
Tonic gen.	*asmā́kam*	*ahmākəm*	*amāxam*
etc.			

No other Indo-European language comes even close to showing so complete and consistent a set of similarities to any one of the Indo-Iranian languages as they show to one another.

Given such closeness in individual features, it is clear that the Indic and Iranian systems must be quite close in general; indeed, on the basis of extant fragments of texts, the grammar of ancient Iranian has been written with the help of the grammar of Sanskrit. Moreover, as has often been observed, the simple application of a few rules of phonological or morphological correspondence permits the transformation of, for example, a passage of the Avesta into an almost correct Vedic text. The vocabularies of the two groups coincide almost completely. Thus, instead of $*k_1$, which provides the initial sound of the word for 'heart' in all the other Indo-European languages (Arm. *sirt,* OSl. *srŭdice,* Lith. *szirdìs,* Gr. καρδίᾱ and κῆρ, Lat. *cor,* OIr. *cride,* Goth. *hairto*), Sanskrit and Iranian have the representatives of a voiced aspirated stop; thus, Skr. *hŕd-* and *hŕdayam,* Av. *zərəd-* and *zərəδaēm,* Pers. *dil.*

It remains quite clear, however, that Indic and Iranian evolved from different Indo-European dialects, whose period of common development was not long enough to effect total fusion. The isoglosses marking the fall of medial *ə (see below, chap. VIII) and the treatment of *wy (chap. IX) pass between Indic and Iranian; Slavic and Iranian share certain lexical features which do not extend to Sanskrit. The two groups, then, though developing along parallel lines, remained to some extent distinct.

There do not appear to be special connections between any particular Iranian dialect and any particular Indic dialect. At first glance, one might attach some importance in this regard to the fact that final *-as becomes -ō both in Sanskrit and the western Prakrits on the one hand, and in the Avesta, which is composed in East Iranian, on the other. But close examination of the facts shows that the Avestan and Sanskrit treatments of *-as are really independent of each other.

Indeed, the Sanskrit development -o (that is, -ō) is peculiar to those cases where -s comes before a following voiced sound. Now, the general law for the treatment of final consonants within an Indo-Iranian phrase is: voiceless element before voiceless element, voiced sound before any voiced sound (stop, sonant, or vowel). This treatment of final consonants differs from that found within a word, in that within the word voiceless elements voice before a voiced stop but remain voiceless before a sonant (vocalic or consonantal) or vowel, e.g.:

medial	final
-asta-	-as ta-
-azda-	-az da-
-asna-	-az na-
-asya-	-az ya-
-asa-	-az a-

or, in those cases where *s* becomes *š* in Indo-Iranian:

-*išta*-	-*iš ta*-
-*ižda*-	-*iž da*-
-*išna*-	-*iž na*-
-*išya*-	-*iž ya*-
-*iša*-	-*iž a*-

Final **-az* before a consonantal element (consonant or consonantal sonant) gives final -*o* in Sanskrit; within a word, **azda* results in Skr. *eda;* before a consonant, **-az* always remains in Iranian in both medial and final position. Thus, at the end of the first term of a compound, i.e., in a position where word-final rules hold true, we find Skr. *ojo-dā́ḥ* 'strength-giving', but Av. *aogaz-dastəma-* 'most strength-giving'. Sanskrit final -*o* from **-az* is thus parallel to Skr. -*ed*- from medial **-azd-,* and it is easy to see that in the eastern Prakrits -*e* occurs in both medial and final position in the word.

Avestan final -*ō* is attributable to different conditions and a different process. It is not a special development but the result of any final **-as,* either within or at the end of a phrase. Unlike Sanskrit, Avestan does not have complicated rules for sandhi; except for words that are closely linked in pronunciation, there is only one development for all cases, and this development does not involve voicing. Wherever *s* shifted to *š,* we find -*iš, -uš, -xš, -fš,* etc.; similarly, **-ts* is represented by -*s,* as in *hąs, stavas, pourutās, gaδōtūs,* etc.; -*ō,* then, does not come from **-az* (ancient development before voiced sounds). Actually, final **-as* changed to -*ah, -h* being the sole result of *s* in Iranian wherever a consonant does not follow immediately, as in -*as ča, -as te;* and, indeed, Old Persian has -*a,* which is to say -*ah,* as its outcome of II. **-as.* Raising of *a* before syllable-final *h* occurs in the Gathas even within a word, as in GAv. *əhmi* from **asmi,* GAv. *məhmaidī* from **masmadi.* The same vowel represents, in the Gathas, final **-ah* from **-as,* always in monosyllables, e.g., *ha̧, ya̧, na̧,* etc., and often in polysyllables, e.g., *vača̧.* Likewise, *ā* occurs as *-āa̧* (resolution of the ligature *å̧*) before final *-h,* so that Av. *-å̧* (i.e., *-āa̧*) corresponds to Skr. final *-āḥ.* Here the development *-å̧ṅha-* from *-āsa-* is in complete conformity with the development from final **-āh* (old **-ās*); and, since **-āsi-, *-āsu-* result in *-āhi-, -āhu-,* it is clear that the raising of *a* is due to the nasal developed after that vowel. This accords with a well-known phenomenon of general phonetics, i.e., that nasalized vowels often tend to be raised; in Avestan itself, **-am* gives *-ąm.* We are thus led to suppose that **-as* changed to **-ah, *-aṅh,* whence **-ō(ṅh).* The development of the nasal arises from the fact that *a* is generally pronounced with the velum barely or not at all raised. Within a word, the nasal passage is not open, however, when *i* or *u* follows, so that **asa* gives *aṅha,* but **asi* and **asu* give *ahi* and *ahu;* and at the end of the word, without any influence to block the development of the nasal, we find *-ō(ṅh)* in all cases. The only difficulty that this explanation offers is that the vowel signs of the text show no trace of closing of *a* before the nasal in *-aṅha-* in medial position. It is known, however, that the addition of vowel signs to the Avesta postdates considerably the composition and recording of the text; moreover, it is easy to see that the influence of the nasal in medial position, i.e., distinct from the preceding vowel, should have been different from its influence in final position, where it merged with the vowel, nasalizing and raising it. We then have, on the one hand, *-aṅha-* and, on the other, **-ąh,* resulting in **-ą̄h* and then *-ō.*

The development *-o* from final **-as* before voiced consonant in Sanskrit and the development *-ō* from any final **-as* in the Avesta are, therefore, two phenomena fundamentally independent of each other.

(Add.) The fact that we find hardly any instances of partial common development in certain Indic and Iranian

idioms, and the consequent lack of any apparent continuity between the two areas, has little probative value,
since in each group we know only a few ancient dialects.

One feature, however, ought to be pointed out in this
regard. All of Indo-Iranian tended to confuse *r* and *l*, but
while the tendency was Indo-Iranian, the confusion was not
manifested everywhere to the same extent. Every IE. *l*
became *r* in Iranian. The same occurrence is to be observed
in the Northwest of India and, consequently, in the Rig-
Veda, which is based on idioms of the Northwest. On the
other hand, initial and intervocalic *l* was preserved in
Indic dialects of other regions. Numerous elements of
these dialects were gradually introduced into the literary
language, which became fixed as Classical Sanskrit. This
explains the appearance of *l* in more recent parts of the
Rig-Veda and its subsequent rise in frequency. Thus, the
root *leubh-* 'love' of OSl. *ljubŭ* 'dear', etc., which is unknown in Iranian and in the early sections of the Rig-Veda,
appears once in Mandala X, with its *l*, in the form *lobháyantī,*
and it is frequent in Classical Sanskrit. The root *$k^w el$-*, as
in Hom. πέλομαι, Cret. τέλεται, etc., is represented in the
Rig-Veda by *cárati,* which is frequent and which concords
with Av. *čaraiti;* but *calati* appears in the Atharva Veda
and subsequently becomes current. In the Rig-Veda, it is
found in reduplicative forms of a popular type: *ávicācaliḥ,*
in Mandala X, and *calācaláḥ,* in a recent section of the great
riddle-hymn (I, 164, 48), which is not of the same character
as the rest of the Rig-Veda. The Rig-Veda has *právate,*
whereas Classical Sanskrit took from East Indic dialects
the form *plávate,* which occurs in the Rig-Veda beginning
with Mandala X. We thus observe an instance of concordance of Iranian with the Indic idioms closest to the
area of Iranian, and discordance with Indic idioms farther
to the East.

From the time of their geographical separation, the
Indic and Iranian dialects evolved along different lines.

Indic retained the voiceless aspirated stops; Iranian lost them. Indic preserved strong articulation of consonants, particularly in initial position; Iranian weakened the consonants, creating numerous voiced and voiceless spirants, and changing initial and intervocalic *s* to *h*. The words of the Indic phrase were linked in pronunciation; those of the Iranian phrase were clearly isolated. Thus the two groups, at first very similar, began to diverge at an early date and were already quite different before the beginning of the Christian Era.

chapter three

Italo-Celtic

FOLLOWING THE PERIOD OF ITALO-CELTIC
unity, the two Italic groups, Latin and Osco-Umbrian,
went through a period of common development, as shown
by a number of striking similarities of detail:

The interrogative–indefinite gave rise to the relative.
The nominative form of the relative is OLat. *quoi* (Lat. *quī*),
Osc. p o i, Umbr. *poi,* as compared with the indefinite
Lat. *quis,* Osc. p i s, Umbr. p i s - i; likewise, Lat. *quid*
and Osc. p i d, on the one hand, and Lat. *quod* and Osc.
pod, on the other, correspond both in form and meaning.

The Osco-Umbrian personal pronouns are uncertain,
but the dative forms are known, and there the parallelism
is complete:

Latin	Oscan	Umbrian
mihī		*mehe*
tibī	t (i) f e i	t e f e *tefe*
sibī	s i f e i	

The 1st-person singular of the verb 'to be' is Lat. *sum,* Osc. s ú m.

Adverb formations are quite similar:

Latin	Oscan	Umbrian
probē(d)	*amprufid*	p r u f e
extrā(d)	e h t r a d	
suprā(d)		*s u b r a*

The present tense of the root **dhē* has the same form, as for example in the 3rd person of the subjunctive: Lat. *faciat,* Osc. f a k i i a d, Umbr. f a ç i a.

The type represented by Skr. *dádhāmi,* Gr. τίθημι, Lith. *dēsti* is not present in this verb, any more than in *iaciō,* as opposed to ἵημι.

The existence of the same denominative formations, as in Lat. *operāri̅,* Osc. ú p s a n n a m, Umbr. *osatu* or Lat. *probāre,* Osc. p r ú f a t t e d, would suffice to indicate a very close relation between Latin and Osco-Umbrian.

There are also semantic phenomena, such as the evolution of the root **deik₁-* from the meaning 'show' to 'say': Lat. *dīcere,* Osc. d e í k u m *deicum,* Umbr. *deitu* '(Lat.) dicito'.

These small common features establish the validity of a period of Italic unity. It is this unity, too, that explains the complete parallelism of the Latin and Osco-Umbrian grammatical systems; just as Sanskrit has helped in the reconstruction of the grammar of ancient Iranian, Latin has helped in the deciphering of the Osco-Umbrian texts — all of them epigraphic — to which no key was provided by any translation. Features common to the two groups are numerous: long vowels are closed; original voiced aspirated stops are represented by voiceless spirants; the spirant **þ* is replaced by *f* (this phenomenon, however, is not Common Italic, as is seen by the contrast between

the dental in Lat. *media* and the *f* in Osc. m e f i ú; there
was a parallel development); intervocalic *s* voices; the nasal
in final position is -*m*, not -*n* as in Greek, Celtic, and
Germanic; short vowels in final syllables tend to fall; the
syntax is the same.

Nevertheless, at the date of their attestation, Oscan
and Umbrian, already quite distinct from each other, show
a much greater difference from Latin than do the ancient
Iranian languages from Sanskrit; never would a pure and
simple Latin transcription of Oscan or Umbrian result
in a correct or even intelligible Latin text. It follows that
the replacement of Osco-Umbrian by Latin was a true
change of language and not an adaptation accomplished
through partial substitutions, such as, for example, the
present-day replacement of French *patois* in the North by
standard literary French.

Before the period of Italic unity, there was a period of
Italo-Celtic unity. This unity, more difficult to grasp, is
not attested by the preservation of a common proper noun
such as that of the Indo-Iranians, or *Aryans*. It is perhaps
to be seen, however, in certain surviving institutions.[1] In
any case, there is no lack of characteristic similarities of a
linguistic nature, viz.,

(1) Shift from $p \ldots k^w$ to $k^w \ldots k^w$, which is regular:

Lat. *quīnque*, Ir. *cōic*, Wel. *pimp*, Bret. *pemp*, Gaul.
πεμπέ(-δουλα) 'cinque(-foil)', in contrast to Gr. πέντε, Skr.
páñca, Arm. *hing*, Lith. *penkì*, etc.

Lat. *coquō*, Wel. *pobi*, in contrast to Skr. *pácati*, OSl. *pekǫ*,
Gr. πέπων, πέσσω.

Lat. *quercus*, *querquētum*, in contrast to OHG. *forha*, OE.
furh. The proper noun Ἑρκύνια, which is Celtic, is not
necessarily in contradiction with this law; the shift from
$*k^wu$ to $*ku$ may antedate the assimilation of initial *p* to
medial k^w, whence the survival of *p* until its disappearance

later together with every Common Celtic *p*. Besides, the
etymology of a proper noun is never very certain.

This law cannot be verified in Osco-Umbrian. We do not
have any way of determining whether the *p* of Osc.
p ú m p e r i a i s '(Lat.) quinturiis', Πομπτιες P ú n t i í s
'(Lat.) Quintius', and of Umbr. p u m p e ř i a s and
p u n t e s 'pentad' is based directly on *p* or on *kʷ*. The
second hypothesis seems certain, a priori. The same
observation applies to the word *popīna* (= Lat. *coquīna*),
which is Latin borrowed from Oscan.

(2) Development of *ar, al* from IE. **ᵒr, *ᵒl*, whereas IE.
*r̥ and **l̥* give It. *or, ol* and Celt. *ri, li*. All neighboring languages have the same vowel in both cases (Gr. αρ and ρα
[or αρ], Germ. *ur*, Lith. *ir* or *ur*, etc.):

Ir. *scaraim* 'I separate', Wel. *ysgar* 'separation', Umbr.
k a r t u '(Lat.) distribuito', k a r u 'portion, flesh', Lat.
carō. Cf. OHG. *scoran*, Lith. *(ăt-)skirai*. This is the root of
OHG. *sceran*, Gr. κείρω, Arm. *kherem*.

Lat. *varus* = Lith. *viras*.

Bryth. *garan* 'crane', Gaul. *(tri-)garanus* '(to the three)
crane(s)'. Cf. Serb. *ždrâl* and *ždrâo* from **žiravŭ*, Gr. γέρανος,
Lith. *gérvė*, OSl. *žeravi̭*, etc.

Wel. *malaf* 'I grind', Umbr. (k u -)m a l t u '(Lat.) com-
molito'. Cf. Arm. *malem* and, with *e*, Ir. *melim*, OSl. *meljǫ;*
with *o*, Goth. *mala*, Lith. *malù;* with *e* or *o*, Lat. *molō*.

Lat. *salix*, Ir. *sail* (gen. *sailech*) is a probative example
only insofar as Gr. ἑλίκη is a cognate. If the Greek word is
not related, nothing proves that the *a* of *salix, sail* and of
OHG. *salaha* is not an original **a*.

Similarly, **ᵒn* gives *an* in Celtic and Italic in various
examples,[2] notably the following:

Lat. *maneō*, in contrast to Gr. μένω, μεμένηκα. Ir. *anaim*
and Bret. *(eh-)anaff* are quite problematic.

Lat. *manus*, Umbr. m a n u v - e 'in the hand', Osc.
manim. Cf. OIce. *mund*.

Ir. *tana,* Bret. *tanau.* Cf. Gr. ταυυ-, ταναός. Lat. *tenuis* has a root with *e,* as does Lith. *tenvas.*

Lat. *canō,* Umbr. k a n e t u, Ir. *canim,* Wel. *canaf.* The grade *e* is not represented in this root, but we find the grade *o* in Gr. κόναβος (and Goth. *hana* 'cock', Lith. *kañklès* a kind of stringed instrument[3]) and the grade *ō* in Lat. *ci-cōnia,* Prænestan *cōnea,* OHG. *huon.*

Nevertheless, this development of *an* from *⁰n* proves little, because, on the one hand, *an* is the result of *$n̥$ in Celtic in most cases (except that Irish has *in* in certain positions) and, on the other, the development is not regular in Latin, where *⁰ni* gives *ini,* e.g., *sine,* cf. Ir. *sain* 'separately', Skr. *sanutár,* Goth. *sundro;* and *cinis,* cf. Gr. κόνις.

(3) Stems in *-o* with genitive in *-ī:* Lat. *virī* = OIr. *fir;* Ogam Ir. *maqi;* Gaul. *Segomari,* genitive of *Segomaros.* The genitive was not preserved in the Brythonic dialects. Osco-Umbrian replaced the form in *-ī* with a form in *-eis* borrowed from *-i*–stems, but it is no doubt for *-ī* that the *-eis* was substituted.

The genitive in *-ī* is extremely characteristic of Italo-Celtic, since it does not appear with any certainty anywhere else[4] and since, with its lack of the thematic vowel *e/o,* which occurs throughout the remainder of the flection, it is completely isolated in the declension of these stems.

(4) Passive in *-r.*[5] The preterite is formed from a single nominal element, the adjective in *-to-:* Lat. *cantātus est,* OIr. *(ro)cēt* 'he was sung (of)', Osc. t e r e m n a t u s t '(Lat.) terminata est'.

Verbs with endings ordinarily of the middle voice took the *-r* of the passive, thus forming the deponent type. This type, with its combination of middle endings and the characteristic *r,* was an innovation peculiar to Italo-Celtic.

It is highly noteworthy that the forms of the 1st person, such as Lat. *loquor* and OIr. *labrur,* are very close.

The Latin type *loquitur* and the Old Irish type *labrithir*, *-labrathar* also have the same structure. In neither Italic nor Celtic is there any trace, in the present tense, of the primary endings in *-tai*, as in Skr. *sácate,* Gr. *ἔπεται* (and Goth. *bairada*); Latin does have *-ai* in the 1st-person singular, e.g., *tutudī* = Skr. *tutude,* but that is a perfect ending. It has been observed that the perfect, in a few cases, generalized middle endings, which may be lost elsewhere; Slavic, retaining no trace of all the middle-voice personal endings in the present, shows *-ĕ* in the sole personal form of the perfect which it has: *vĕdĕ* 'I know'; and, since instead of this perfect the other languages use the active form (Skr. *véda,* Gr. *ϝοῖδα,* Goth. *wait*), OSl. *vĕdĕ* points to a generalization of the middle form throughout the Slavic perfect at a prehistoric period. Old Irish, similarly, has only deponent endings in the 1st- and 3rd-persons plural of certain of its preterites.

The 1st-person plural, Lat. *loquimur,* OIr. *labrimmir,* *-labrammar,* has nothing to do with the middle ending in Skr. *-mahi,* GAv. *-maidī,* Gr. *-μεθα,* and is based on the 1st person of the active voice. The 2nd-person plural, borrowed in Latin from a nominal form (*loquiminī*), does not differ in Irish from the active forms: OIr. *labrithe, -labraid.* In the matter of the deponent, then, the similarity between Italic and Irish holds true to the smallest detail. The deponent was clearly a common innovation.[6]

(5) Irish and Latin have two subjunctive forms which are common to them and peculiar to them. One such correspondence would in itself be characteristic; the existence of two has a value comparable to that of the innovation of the deponent. The features are:

(a) Endings with *-ā-,* e.g., Lat. *feram,* OIr. *bera* (and corresponding forms in Osco-Umbrian).[7]

(b) Endings with *-s-,* e.g., OIr. *tīasu, tēis,*[8] Lat. *dīxim, faxim* (and *dīxō, faxō*). First, the type *faxim* clearly has no connection, either in form or in meaning, with the system of the perfectum, into which it has often — and incorrectly — been incorporated; and *dīxim* is hardly the same thing as *dīxerim.* These subjunctives in *-s-* do not show the characteristics of the corresponding presents and do constitute independent stems; thus we have Lat. *faxim, faxō* in contrast to *faciō, ausim* in contrast to *audeō* and, likewise, OIr. *-ges* in contrast to *guidim* 'I pray'. Secondly, the *-s-*subjunctive provides the Oscan future tense of the type f u s t. There might be some temptation to see a relation between the future of the type *faxō* and the Greek future, between *dīxō* and δείξω, for example; however, the resemblance is undoubtedly fortuitous, since the Latin future in general is based on early subjunctive forms; furthermore, what happens in Latin can obviously not be isolated from what happens in Irish. Moreover, the Indo-European future appears only in those languages having a future participle, viz., Indo-Iranian, Baltic, Greek, and, to some extent, Slavic; to judge by Vedic, the participle was the principal form of the Indo-European future.

The Italic future of derived verbs, such as Lat. *amābō, monēbō, audībō,* Fal. *carefo, pipafo,* corresponds exactly to the Irish future in *-b* and *-f-*. This connection has been disputed, but for reasons that do not seem wholly valid.

It is essential to note that the Italo-Celtic subjunctive in *-ā-* or in *-s-* is independent both of the present stem (Latin infectum) and of the preterite stem. Old Latin, for example, has *advenam* alongside *veniō, vēnī,* and Old Irish has *-bia* alongside *benaim.*

(6) Formation of the superlative: Lat. *maximus,* Osc. n e s s i m a s '(Lat.) proximae', Umbr. *nesimei,* OIr. *nessam,* Wel. *nesaf;* and the type Lat. *facillimus,* Gaul. Οὐξισαμη, OIr. *dīlem.* The other Indo-European languages show a different formation, as in Skr. *svádiṣṭhaḥ,* Gr. ἥδιστος, OHG. *suozisto.*

(7) The suffix *-tei-* is supplemented by a nasal suffix, as in Lat. *nātiō, natiōnis,* Umbr. *natine* (ablative), OIr. *toimtiu* (gen. *toimten*) 'thought'. Armenian, too, has a form *-uthiwn* (gen. *-uthean*), but this is a complex suffix peculiar to Armenian, whereas the Italic and Celtic features coincide perfectly.

(8) Vocabulary is identical in part; this is true of some very important words, particularly prepositions and preverbs:

Lat. *dē* = Ir. *dī,* Bryth. *di;* Lat. *cum* = Ir. *com* (and *co-* = *co*).
Or, again: Lat. *īmus,* cf. Ir. *ís* 'below' and *īsel,* Wel. *isel.*
Or, in the case of substantives: Lat. *pectus,* Ir. *ucht* (gen. *ochta*); Lat. *terra,* Ir. *tír* (stem in *-es-*[9]); Lat. *veru,* Umbr. b e r u s (abl. plur.), OIr. *bir,* Bryth. *ber.*[10]

The adjective Lat. *crispus,* Wel. *crych* (same meaning), Gaul. *Crixos* (proper noun) is peculiar to Italo-Celtic.

The original nouns for 'son' and 'daughter' disappeared and were replaced by new words: Lat. *fīlius* and *fīlia,* Ir. *macc* (Ogam gen. *maqqi* and *maqi*), Bryth. *map* 'son' and Ir. *ingen* (Ogam *inigena*) 'daughter'. Lat. *fīlius* and *fīlia* are derived from the notion of 'feeding', and the Celtic word **mak^{w}k^{w}o-,* with its double consonant, seems to belong to the speech of children.

The demonstrative of distant object (i.e., 3rd-person demonstrative) is marked by *l-* only in Italic and, in part, Celtic.[11]

We must nevertheless not exaggerate the importance of these lexical correspondences. The list of strong verbs in Irish,[12] for example, coincides only minimally with that of the Latin strong verbs.

The general resemblance of the grammar of Italic and that of Celtic remains appreciable, though it tends to be concealed by the numerous and extensive changes that each of the two groups underwent independently. The

Irish grammar with which we are forced to compare the grammar of Latin is, besides, that of a language attested many centuries after Latin and consequently at a more advanced stage of development; comparison is thereby rendered difficult and imprecise.

Just as Indo-Iranian unity does not prevent isoglosses from passing between Sanskrit and Iranian, Italo-Celtic unity does not prevent isoglosses from passing between Italic and Celtic. Thus, as will be seen below, there are several features common to Greek and Italic that are not present in Celtic.

There is a particular similarity of Osco-Umbrian and Celtic in the treatment of labiovelars: $*g^w$ gives b in both Osco-Umbrian and Celtic. However, while the feature is common to both groups, it is almost surely the result of an independent development within each group; indeed, k^w at first remained q (attested in the Ogam inscriptions) and then became k in Gaelic. Moreover, the labialization of labiovelars is a perfectly natural phenomenon, one that is found independently in Greek as well, and that other languages, too, have shown at various dates; it is to be observed, for example, among the Neo-Latin languages, in Romanian.

(Add.) A. Walde, *Über älteste Beziehungen zwischen Kelten und Italikern* (Innsbruck, 1917), is not very convincing. Walde believes that Brythonic has special ties with Osco-Umbrian, and Gaelic with Latin. However, his thesis is defeated by the obvious unity of the Italic group on the one hand and of the Celtic group on the other. His arguments, moreover, have little probative value.

The change of $*k^w$ to p could have taken place independently in Brythonic and in Osco-Umbrian, just as it took place independently in Greek and in Romanian. If, furthermore, as far as the voiceless sound is concerned, the shift did not occur in Gaelic, it is because of a special difficulty arising from the absence of *p* in Celtic; as for the voiced sound, Gaelic has *b* for *$*g^w$*, just as Brythonic has. The special situation of Gaelic in the matter of *$*k^w$* no doubt stems from the fact that Gaelic tends toward voiceless pronunciation: initial *w* tends toward *f*, not *g^w* as in Brythonic, and intervocalic *t* tends toward þ, not *d;* thus it is that the element *^{w}* of voiceless *k^w* was less operative in Gaelic than in Brythonic.

The absence of the deponent in Brythonic may arise from the fact that the Brythonic dialects are known only at an advanced stage in their development. In Irish, which is more archaic, the deponent becomes increasingly rare in the course of the historical period. As for Osco-Umbrian, the lack of examples of the deponent may be accidental: we possess only a few texts. Moreover, Umbr. *persnimu* has always been interpreted as a deponent, comparable to Lat. *precātor,* and Walde's rejection of this example is wholly unwarranted. The stage in which Brythonic is known to us is comparable to the Romance stage of Latin; it is to be noted that the Romance languages do not possess the deponent.

chapter four

Balto-Slavic

THE GENERAL RESEMBLANCE OF BALTIC AND Slavic is so apparent that no one challenges the notion of a period of common development. Nevertheless, upon close examination the innovations and the individual features common to the two groups are less probative than they appear at first.

For a proper evaluation of the situation, we must begin by noting two general facts:

First, Baltic and Slavic are the descendants of almost identical Indo-European dialects. No important isogloss divides Baltic from Slavic, i.e., Baltic and Slavic are never found on opposite sides of the lines marking the boundaries of the features by which the dialects of Common Indo-European are distinguished. So total a measure of sameness is not found, as we have seen, at the Indo-European origin of either Indo-Iranian or Italo-Celtic.

Secondly, Baltic and Slavic show the common trait of never having undergone in the course of their develop-

ment any sudden systemic upheaval. Indo-Iranian fused
the vowels *e* and *o* with *a* and thus threw the system of
vocalic gradation into confusion. Greek eliminated intervocalic -*s*- and -*y*- and radically simplified the declensional
system, particularly by eliminating those cases with "real"
value and preserving only the "grammatical" cases, viz.,
nominative, vocative, accusative, genitive, and dative. The
Latin sound-system was upset by initial accentuation.
There is nothing of a similar nature to be found in Slavic
or Baltic; there is no indication of a serious dislocation of
any part of the linguistic system at any time. The sound
structure has in general remained intact to the present;
even intervocalic consonants, which everywhere else have
undergone some degree of change, have remained almost
untouched in Baltic and Slavic. Baltic and Slavic are consequently the only languages in which certain modern
word-forms resemble those reconstructed for Common
Indo-European. Lithuanian *gývas* 'living' or *ěsti* 'he is',
Russ. *pekú* 'I cook', *sěmená* 'seed' or *nová* 'new' still have the
general appearance of the Indo-European words that they
represent.

With an identical point of departure, with no subsequent
systematic deviation, with their development in adjacent
regions and under similar cultural conditions — Baltic and
Slavic could hardly fail to show a great overall resemblance
to each other. This likeness is, moreover, accentuated by
the fact that most of the words borrowed by Baltic come
from Slavic; their similarity in vocabulary and even in
word formation, great at the beginning, became even
greater later on.

We may now review the main arguments advanced in
favor of the reality of Balto-Slavic unity, and attempt to
determine whether they are sufficient to establish a period
of common development postdating Indo-European unity.

K. Brugmann—*Kurze vergleichende Grammatik der indogermanischen Sprachen* (Strasbourg, 1902-04), §11—makes the
following observations:

(1) The vocalic liquids and nasals *$r̥$, *$l̥$, *$n̥$, and *$m̥$ gave
Baltic *ir, il, in,* and *im* (or *ur, ul, un,* and *um*);Common
Slavic has *$^ir̥$, *$^il̥$, and *ę* (or *$^ur̥$, *$^ul̥$, and *ŭ*). The similarity
is a real one; it does not mean, however, that Baltic and
Slavic had a common development subsequent to the Indo-
European period. For it seems that the glide vowel was
fixed as early as the Indo-European stage, and that we are
concerned here with a dialectal phenomenon of Indo-
European time. To be sure, most of the languages differ
in this respect; still, Greek and Armenian are alike in
having *a* as the glide vowel. And with the nasals the same
vowel appears in Indo-Iranian: *$n̥$ is represented by II. *a,*
Gr. *α,* Arm. *an,* and *$m̥$ by II. *a,* Gr. *α,* Arm. *am.* High
vowels, *i* and *u,* appear, on the contrary, in Celtic (for *$r̥$
and *$l̥$, giving *ri* and *li*), in Germanic (*ur, ul, un, um*), in
Baltic, and in Slavic. What we have here, then, is the
general outline of an Indo-European dialect grouping that
is hard to see in detail.

Particularly in the case of Balt. *ŭr, ŭl* and Sl. *$^ŭr̥$, *$^ŭl̥$,
the origin of the *u* is surely Indo-European, as noted; *u*
appears even in languages that ordinarily developed other
vowels in glide position, e.g.,

OSl. *krŭma* (Russ. *kormá*) 'stern (of a vessel)'; cf. Gr.
πρύμνη.

Lith. *surbù* 'suck'; cf. Lesb. *ῥυφέω.*

OSl. *grŭlo* (Russ. *górlo,* Serb. *gr̂lo*), Lith. *gurklỹs* (acc.
gùrklį); cf. Lat. *gurges.* Similarly, *^ol is represented by *ul*
in words of the same family: Lat. *gula,* Arm. *e-kul* 'he
swallowed'. (The *u* of Arm. *ekul* is most likely not based
on an original *$ō$.)

Examples of this kind are few and their exact value cannot be determined, but they suffice at least to establish

that the glide vowel began to be fixed in Indo-European itself. As late as Sanskrit, IE. $*\underset{\circ}{r}$ and $*\underset{\circ}{l}$ are represented by $\underset{\circ}{r}$, which is short, and $*\underset{\circ}{n}$ and $*\underset{\circ}{m}$ are represented in Indo-Iranian by short ă, in Greek by short ă. Indo-European $*\underset{\circ}{r}$ must have been something quite close to what certain Hindu grammarians describe as the pronunciation of Skr. ṛ: a quarter-vowel + r + a quarter-vowel — extremely short vocalic elements whose timbre was far from clear because of the minimal duration of the sound, but was nonetheless already somewhat defined in the Indo-European dialects. The vowel, as we have seen, tended to differ from region to region. The parallelism of Balt. *ir* and Sl. $*^{i}r$, Balt. *ur* and Sl. $*^{u}r$, etc., goes back, then, to the period of Common Indo-European.

(2) Neither Baltic nor Slavic shows double consonants. However, this is the result of a Common Indo-European tendency. In Baltic and Slavic the tendency to eliminate such consonants remained operative and reached its natural conclusion. The same development undoubtedly occurred in Armenian where, before the fall of *i* and *u* and the borrowing of certain foreign words, there seem to have been no double consonants. The other languages did not maintain the Indo-European tendency. So far as Indo-European is concerned, we know that double consonants were of minimal importance; most of those encountered appear in terms of affection and children's words — the type, for example, of Gr. γύννις [1] or OHG. *zocchōn* [2] or the type of Gr. ἄττα, 'dad(dy)', Lat. *atta*, Skr. *attā*, Goth. *atta*, OHG. *atto*, OIr. *aite* (with a *t* and not a *th*, hence originally *tt*). Apart from these quite special cases, Indo-European tended to eliminate double consonants. We shall see below (chap. VII) how *-tt-*, often brought about morphologically, underwent various dialectal developments in Indo-European. The double consonant *-ss-* was eliminated in Indo-European itself in the well-known example Skr. *ási*, Av.

ahi, Gr. εἶ, contrasting with Hom. ἐσσι, OLat. *ess* (revealed metrically), Arm. *es;* Indo-Iranian also has as locative plural for *-es*–stems Skr. *-asu,* Av. *-ahu,* instead of the expected form *-as-su.* The elimination of double consonants, then, had its origin in Indo-European itself.

(3) The Lithuanian definite adjective *geràs-is* is entirely comparable to OSl. *dobrŭ-jĭ* (*dobryjĭ*). Yet the two types are not quite the same in detail and do not have the same importance in the two languages. Above all, the use of the stem **yo-,* on which these juxtapositional adjectives are based, is found too in the Avesta, except that its placement is different; *tāiš šyaoθanāiš yāiš vahištāiš* (Y. XXXV, 4) 'by these excellent actions' represents a normal Avestan type. The essential fact is the agreement in case between **yo-* and the noun and adjective. This agreement takes place in Iranian no less than Baltic and Slavic.

(4) Masculine active participles changed to the **-yo-*inflection; thus Lith. gen. sg. *vēžanczio* = OSl. *vezǫšta.* The shift resulted from the influence of feminine forms in **-yā-,* which are Indo-European; it was a quite natural shift, an exact equivalent of which occurs in West Germanic: OE. *berende,* OSax. *berandi,* OHG. *beranti.* This change was only one consequence of a general innovation, i.e., adjectives tended earlier than nouns to take endings of the vocalic type. Lithuanian has only *-a*–stem and *-u*–stem adjectives; Slavic, more advanced, has only *-o*–stems, with the corresponding feminine form. One might argue the preservation of the early masculine nominative singulars, e.g., Lith. *vežās,* OSl. *vezy;* but Gothic, in which the participle, under the influence of the comparative, shifted to stems in *-n-,* also preserved the nominative singular of the type *bairands* (alongside *bairanda*).

(5) The intercalation of *-i-* in forms such as Lith. *akmen-i-mìs* and OSl. *kamen-i-mŭ* is in no way characteristic, for such intercalations are found also in Lat. *ped-i-bus* (in

which the *-i-*, it is true, is ambiguous and may represent any short vowel), Arm. *ot-i-wkh,* etc. Furthermore, in both Baltic and Slavic, the sameness of the singular and plural accusatives of *-i-*stems and consonant stems came about phonetically, thus facilitating the convergence of the two series (which, however, could have taken place otherwise).

(6) The demonstrative stems **to-* and **tā-* replaced the early forms of the type Skr. *sá* and *sâ,* Gr. ὁ and ἥ, Goth. *sa* and *so,* with the analogical forms Lith. *tàs* and *tà,* OSl. *tŭ* and *ta.* However, this was a very simple innovation, resulting from the common tendency toward normalization that is shown by both Baltic and Slavic. Old Saxon has, likewise, *thē* and *thia;* Old High German has *der* and *diu.*

(7) The datives Lith. *manei, mán,* OPruss. *mennei* do not correspond to OSl. *mině* in the vocalism of either the first or the second syllable. The Slavic and Baltic forms here provide a fine example of the parallel, but independent, innovations that characterize the two groups.

(8) The genitive–ablative singular Lith. *vilko* is the same as OSl. *vlĭka,* and both correspond to the Sanskrit ablative *vṛkāt.* This confusion of genitive and ablative results from the fact that, in all types other than the thematic type, the genitive and ablative singulars have one and the same form. Greek used the genitive of *-o*–stems for the ablative; Baltic and Slavic did the reverse. It is not at all evident that this occurrence can be traced back to a period of common development, for Old Prussian, with its genitive *deiwas,* shows no connection with it. The demonstratives are widely divergent: Lithuanian uses the original ablative *tō* for the genitive, but Old Prussian has *stesse* (original genitive, cf. Skr. *tásya,* Hom. τοῖο) and Slavic has the new form *togo.* While the Italo-Celtic form with *-ī,* altogether unique, is very important, the generalization of the ablative, which is easy to explain as an independent development, proves nothing.

The above phenomena establish only that Baltic and Slavic underwent parallel developments; this parallelism had as a natural consequence the creation of a few identical forms, but these like innovations do not point to any period of common development. A good example of the parallel and independent innovations characterizing these languages is provided by their shift of accent from a circumflex element to a following acute, which Saussure discovered in Lithuanian and which also occurs in Old Prussian and in the Slavic dialects. The shift came about independently in Lithuanian, Old Prussian, and Slavic. In regard to Lithuanian and Old Prussian, their independence is indicated by the fact—noted by A. Bezzenberger, *KZ,* XLI, 74—that Old Prussian shifted the accent from a circumflex long to a following acute, but not from a short to a following acute; thus we have OPruss. *antrā, imtā, piencktā,* but *maddla, tikra* (in contrast to Lith. *tikrà*), *wissa* (in contrast to Lith. *visà*). As for Slavic, the value of the observation [by Meillet], *MSL,* XI, 350, has been disputed by H. Pedersen, *KZ,* XXXVIII, 335, but the objection does not seem convincing; see [Meillet] *Archiv für slavische Philologie,* XXV, 426. W. Vondrák[3] sees the Serbian type *kòpām* as resulting from the secondary return of the accent to the initial syllable, and it is upon this backward shift of the accent, granted by Saxmatov,[4] that Kulbakin[5] bases his objections, too. According to Kulbakin, we should have **ȍd jezȳkā, *zȁpitāš,* because the accent is not maintained on a medial syllable with circumflex intonation. It is impossible to present here a detailed examination of accentuation in the groups preposition + noun and preverb + verb, but it is by no means clearly demonstrated that it may be traced to phonetic causes; see [Meillet] *IF,* XXI, 341. Moreover, Serb. *pòhvālȋš,* which never underwent contraction, behaves exactly as does *zàpȳtāš,* which did, and nothing gives us grounds for challenging the antiquity of the accentuation of Serb. *hvâliš*. As for the *ĕ* in *jĕzikā*, which is phonetically incorrect, it is clearly explained by all the other cases in which there is short *e*, such as gen. sg. *jĕzika*, etc.

It is hard to see, then, that any decisive objection has been raised to the demonstration of the dialectal nature of this accent shift.

Even apart from borrowings, the vocabularies of Slavic and Baltic show numerous cognates — more precisely, cognates that are found nowhere else or cognates that in Baltic and Slavic have a form different from their form in other languages.

Among the words that are not found elsewhere, we may cite the following: OSl. *blŭxa* = Lith. *blusà; lipa* (Russ. *lípa*, Serb. *lȉpa*, Cz. *lípa*) = Lith. *lĕpa; dzvĕzda* (Pol. *gwiazda*), cf. Lith. *zvaigzdĕ̃*, OPruss. *swāigstan; glava* (originally oxytonic in the nominative, which condition brought about a change in the root intonation), cf. Lith. *galvà (gálvą)*, OPruss. *gallū; rąka* = *rankà*, OPruss. *ranco* (cf. Lith. *renkiù*); *rogŭ* = *rāgas*, OPruss. *rags; alŭkati (lakati)*, cf. Lith. *álkti*, OPruss. *alkĩns; metą*, cf. Lith. *metù* and *metati, mĕtati*, cf. Lett. *mētāt; ladĭji* (Russ. *lód'ja*, Pol. *łodzia*, Serb. *lâđa*), cf. Lith. *eldijà*.[6] The concordance of a noun such as the one for 'iron' — OSl. *želĕzo* (Russ. *žel'ĕzo*, Serb. *žĕljezo*, Pol. *želazo*), Lith. *geležìs*, OPruss. *gelso* (see Leskien, "Bildung", p. 234) — shows that such lexical agreements must to a great extent be attributable to a common culture, for this last example designates an object that had no name in Indo-European.

There are many words which have cognates in the other Indo-European languages, but whose form in Baltic and Slavic is not exactly duplicated elsewhere, e.g., OSl. *aba*, Lith. *abù*, OPruss. *abbai* (in contrast to Gr. *ἄμφω*, Lat. *ambō*; Skr. *ubhaú*, GAv. *ubā*; Goth. *bai*); *ovĭnŭ, āvinas, awins; nogŭtĭ, nagùtis, naguts; zemlja, žĕmĕ, semmē; zvĕrĭ, zvĕrìs, swīrins* (acc. pl.); *vrata, vartaĩ, warto; plušta* (Slov. *pljuča*), *plaūcziai, plauti;*

rataji̯, ártojis, artoys; smrŭdĕti, smirdĕti; nagŭ, nůgas; milŭ, mēlas; visi̯ (from **visŭ*), *visas, wissas; zima, žēmà; sladŭkŭ, saldùs* (cf. Arm. *khaɫer* 'soft'); *sivŭ, szývas, sĩwan; jis* and *jiz* (Pol. *s, z*), *isz; vydra, údra* (both in words with *ū*); *vetŭxŭ, vetuszas; večerŭ, vãkaras; ziždą, žēdžiu.* This list, significant in itself, could easily be lengthened.

Often, however, we also find the same words with slight variants, going back to the Indo-European period; for example, Slavic has *dĭni̯* and Lithuanian *dënà;* Slavic has *dvi̯ri* and Lithuanian *dùrys,* etc. In addition, although Slavic and Lithuanian show *osmŭ = ãšmas* 'eighth', the parallelism of OSl. *sedmŭ* 'seventh' with Lith. *sēkmas* and OPruss. *septmas* nevertheless supposes an initial difference at the Indo-European stage, as proved by Gr. ἕβδομος. 'Shoulder' is Lith. *petỹs* (root of Gr. πετάννῡμι) and OSl. *pleště* (root of Gr. πλατύς, ὠμοπλάτη): the process is the same, and so is the suffix, but the nouns are different.

We conclude that Baltic and Slavic had identical points of departure and that they developed under the same conditions and influences. There may even have been some period of common development, but, if so, neither Baltic nor Slavic, the most conservative of the Indo-European languages, produced any notable innovations in the course of it. It is sufficient to examine the verb system to see that the two developments were independent at an early date. Basically, everything is the same: the same two stems, the same general structure. The details, however, are quite distinct. The preterites are completely different; the nasal element in those verbs containing such an element is a suffix in Slavic, but an infix in Baltic; the *i* of the type *mĭnitŭ* is long in Slavic, while the *i* of the type *mìni* is short in Lithuanian; and so on. Baltic and Slavic provide a fine example of two parallel, but long autonomous, developments.[7]

chapter five

The Gutturals

THE GUTTURAL THEORY IS TOO WELL KNOWN to be summarized here. If we set aside what remains in dispute, it is now established that, corresponding to a labiovelar such as Lat. *qu,* Indo-Iranian, for example, has a pure guttural, *k* (or *č* before a prepalatal), and that, corresponding to a palatalized prepalatal (modified by the palatalization) such as Skr. *j,* Av. *z,* Arm. *c,* etc., Latin has a pure guttural, *g.* From this point of view, Slavic, Baltic, Armenian (together with Phrygian and Thracian), and Albanian belong to the same type as Indo-Iranian; and Greek, Italic, Celtic, and Germanic (as well, no doubt, as Illyrian) belong to the same type as Latin. In the matter of guttural types, then, the Indo-European languages divide into an Eastern group and a Western group. The two phonological developments always go together, and the isoglosses delimiting their respective areas are consequently of great importance, for they coincide perfectly. This total concordance is, to be sure, attributable to the fact that the two phenomena are connected and, to some extent, reciprocally conditioned; but it is nonetheless meaningful.

To these two concordant phenomena, another must be added. Besides Lat. c = Skr. ς and Skr. k (c) = Lat. qu, there is a third: Skr. k (c) = Lat. c.

However this fact may be interpreted — whether one posits a third series of gutturals (which is the simplistic hypothesis of most linguists) or tries to explain the correspondence on the basis of special circumstances (as has been attempted by C. Bartholomae, then by the author of the present work, and, finally, by H. Hirt) — there is in any case a third isogloss that coincides exactly with the first two. The treatment of gutturals is a unified treatment in each of the groups under consideration, and there is no overlapping.

In order to determine the significance of this set of isoglosses, we must first know which was the innovating side. It is easy to see how k^w can lose its labial quality and become $k;$ the phenomenon occurs in each of the Western dialects under certain special conditions; indeed, one of the Celtic dialects, Gaelic, has only c (i.e., k) as representative of the original Western $*k^w$, and Celtic in general seems to show West IE. $*g^wh$ as g. It is also easy to see how a prepalatal in clearly frontal articulation can spontaneously undergo alterations of the type Skr. j, Arm. c and Av. z, Lith. $\check{z}$, Sl. z, etc. Arabic, for example, has j for the Semitic $g;$ the Armenian dialect of Karabagh shows an analogous evolution in early times.[1] The modification of the prepalatals is already at a very advanced stage in the attested forms of the Eastern group, as in the voiceless sounds Skr. ς, Av. s, OSl. s, Lith. sz, Arm. s, etc., but we can detect forms even more archaic. Sanskrit has k for the original prepalatal before s which becomes $\check{s}$; thus, the 2nd person of $v\acute{e}\varsigma mi$ is $v\acute{e}k\d{s}i$. In Slavic, when a word has s in medial

position, the prepalatal, through dissimilation, becomes a
guttural, e.g., OSl. *gǫsì* in contrast to Lith. *žąsìs*. Sanskrit *j*
and Arm. *c* for the voiced consonant and Arm. *j* for the
voiced aspirate attest, if not the first stage (*ǵ*) of the prepalatal, at least the second stage, that of the affricate, which
surprisingly is not preserved for the voiceless consonant.
Finally, the Persian development of *θ* (voiceless dental
spirant) and *d* also goes back, necessarily, to the affricate
articulation that must have been at a certain period the
articulation of the early prepalatals in all the Eastern dialects; the same is true of some Albanian developments.

It is among the Eastern dialects, then, that we find
common innovation. The grouping of Indo-Iranian,
Armenian, Slavic, Baltic, and Albanian, all of which
introduced a change in the same direction, is thereby
firmly established. The grouping of Greek, Italic, Celtic,
and Germanic is less solidly proved, since in the case of
the gutturals (the only case considered in this chapter)
these languages basically preserve the pre-Indo-European
situation.

The Eastern dialects tend to show agreement of the
point of articulation of the gutturals with that of the
following vowel, e.g., *ko,* but *ke*. The natural result of this
tendency is affricate pronunciation of the prepalatals thus
produced. We observe it regularly in Indo-Iranian and
Slavic; it is not, however, a general Eastern phenomenon,
for, while Lettish shows it, the other two Baltic dialects,
Lithuanian and Old Prussian, keep the prepalatal stop;
and, while Armenian represents the **ǵh* of Eastern **ǵhe,*
*ǵhi by *je, ji,* it regularly preserves *ke* from **ǵe* (as in *e-ker*
'he ate') and *khe* from **ke* (as in *kherem* 'I flay, I scrape');
ǯ may always be based on *ky,* as in *ačkh* 'eyes' (cf. Hom. ὄσσε).
All the more may we affirm that the Hellenic opposition
of τε from **kʷe* and πο from **kʷo* has nothing to do with

the Indo-Iranian and Slavic developments: an examination of Greek itself suffices to show as much, for certain Greek dialects show π before mid front vowels, as in Aeol. πήλυι as opposed to τῆλε in the other dialects, or Aeol. πέσσαρες, Boeot. πέτταρες as opposed to Dor. τέτορες, Att. τέτταρες, Ion. τέσσερες. Besides, dentalization of the labiovelars takes place in Greek only before mid front vowels, and not before ι (as shown by βιός 'bow', ὄφις, etc.), a fact which establishes an essential distinction between the Greek and Indo-Iranian developments. Finally, the shift to affricate pronunciation takes place both for the gutturals corresponding to Western pure gutturals and for those corresponding to Western labiovelars; Greek κ, γ, χ corresponding to Eastern pure gutturals are never dentalized, thus Gr. γέρανος in contrast to OSl. žeravĭ.

If, like H. Hirt and the author of the present work, one accepts basing the correspondence–type Eastern *k, *g, *gh = Western *k, *g, *gh on *k₁, *g₁, *g₁h influenced by preceding or following sounds, then one sees that the tendency, in pronouncing the gutturals, to give them the point of articulation of the adjacent sounds is ancient in the Eastern group. And it is indeed noteworthy that more or less clear traces of the prepalatal pronunciation of the gutturals before prepalatal vowels are found, as has just been seen, in all the Eastern groups.

There is an area in which Armenian curiously coincides with Greek (and perhaps other Western dialects as well). After u, Greek shows no labiovelars, except under the influence of analogy; Saussure has thus explained the contrast of αἰ-πόλος, οἰο-πόλος, ἀμφί-πολος with βου-κόλος; Greek also has εὔχομαι in contrast to Lat. voveō, Umbr. v u f e t e s '(Lat.) consecratis' and GAv. aogǝdā 'he said'. Likewise, after u, Armenian has only the representatives

of the early prepalatals, as in Arm. *usanim* 'I learn' in
contrast to OSl. *vyknǫti, učiti.* As striking as it may be, this
likeness may be fortuitous. On the one hand, the Greek
development is, in fact, disputed;[2] and, if it is authentic,
it seems to have come about after the establishment of the
autonomy of Greek; for we find κύκλος in contrast to Skr.
cakrám, Lith. *kāklas,* OE. *hweogol, hweohhol,* which is to say
that an ϝ created in Greek itself had this effect on a following *kʷ.* On the other hand, Armenian has *awcanem* 'I rub
with oil' alongside Skr. *anákti* and Lat. *unguō,* and *awj*
'serpent' alongside Lith. *angìs,* Lat. *anguis* — alongside, in
other words, the representatives of the original prepalatals
after a diphthong in *u,* where the *u* comes, by some obscure
process, from an Indo-European nasal. If we were nevertheless to accept the connection of the Armenian phenomenon with the supposed Greek one, the result would
be a secondary isogloss intersecting the great isogloss of
guttural development.

The shift of the labiovelars to labial articulation takes
place in a large segment of the Western dialects, but it
shows separate realization in each one. Greek has τ before
mid front vowels. Of the Italic dialects, Oscan and Umbrian
show labialization, but Latin lacks it completely. In Celtic,
Irish has *c* to represent original **kʷ,* and voiced aspirated
*gʷh is represented by *g* in Common Celtic, as Osthoff
has seen. Germanic, finally, has the labial only under
certain special conditions and normally keeps the labiovelars. The labialization of labiovelars, then, does not
have the character of a Western dialectal phenomenon; its
frequency indicates only that Western pronunciation of the
labiovelars was of such a nature as to facilitate this kind
of change. Besides, the labiovelars seem to have been a
rather unstable phonetic element. The Eastern dialects
eliminated them even at the Indo-European stage; and,

whether through a shift to velar articulation or through reduction to pure gutturals (as in Vulgar Latin, whence Fr. *qui,* Itn. *chi,* etc., in contrast to Lat. *quī*), the Western dialects in their turn eliminated them in the course of a more or less advanced period of their evolution; today only a few Germanic dialects still have *qu,* from IE. *g^w.

chapter six

The Vowels *o* and *a*

CELTIC, ITALIC, GREEK, AND ARMENIAN (together with Phrygian) regularly distinguish between *ŏ* and *ă;* they fall together only in certain special cases, few in number, rigorously defined and varying from one language to another. Corresponding to these two distinct vowels, the other dialects show only one vowel, *a* in Germanic, Albanian, Baltic, and Indo-Iranian, and *o* in Slavic. This isogloss intersects that of the gutturals; Armenian goes together with Greek, Italic, and Celtic, while Germanic goes along with Albanian, Baltic, Slavic, and Indo-Iranian. And not surprisingly: the lines marking dialect boundaries are all independent of one another, as will be shown in the course of this work.

With its *o*, Slavic seems to be set apart from the other languages of the same group, but the vowel is not necessarily ancient. Immediately before the historical period, Slavic had a short *ŏ* which served as both *o* and *a;* in borrowings, for example, this *o* rendered *o* and *a* of the

adjacent languages (Greek, Germanic, and Latin), as in
sobota 'Saturday'. Conversely, Greek authors of the seventh
century quite often rendered Slavic *o* by Greek α, as has
been shown by P. Kretschmer (*Archiv für slavische Philologie*,
XXVII, 128). Vasmer (*KZ*, XLI, 157) has pointed out
Kretschmer's exaggeration of the importance of his findings, but he has not reduced their value to nothing, and
it remains a fact that in the seventh century Slavic *o* was a
vowel whose timbre lay somewhere between *o* and *a*. In
popular borrowings, Gr. α is rendered — under conditions
we need not explore here — by Sl. *o* or *a*, as in OSl. *korablji*
from Gr. καράβιον (or rather καράβιν). An original *a* could
easily have given such an *o*, and there is no reason to set
Slavic apart from the other languages to whose group it
belongs.

There is a detail that lends support to the idea that Sl.
o represents *ŭ* of Common Slavic. The diphthong **ei*
merged completely with *ī*, in Slavic as in Germanic. And,
just as in Germanic, the diphthong **ou* or **au* (Sl. *u*) remained distinct from **ū* (Sl. *y*), the shift from **ū* to Sl. *y*
being recent moreover, since Slavic words borrowed from
Germanic participated in the shift. If the treatment of the
u–diphthong is not parallel to that of *ei*, it is because of
the greater degree of aperture of the first component and
because of the necessity of starting with **au* rather than
*ou. It is clear, besides, that the diphthong **au* (whence
*ou, ū) was long maintained in Slavic, for *j* does not change
it: **jy* becomes *ji*, but *ju* (from **jau*, then **jou*) survives,
as does *ją*.

The vowels *ō* and *ā* are distinct in the same dialects that
distinguish between *ŏ* and *ă*. It is to be noted, however,
that, in the Celtic dialects, accented *ō* becomes *ā*. Since the
accent is not in the same position in the various dialects of
the group, the *ā* also is found in different positions; thus
the Brythonic *ā* in OWel. *petguar*, Bret. *pevar* (cf. Goth.

fidwor) is not duplicated in Irish, where the accent falls on
the initial syllable. In Albanian, *ō* and *ā* remain distinct,
with *ō* represented by *e* and *ā* by *o*. Finally, in Letto-
Lithuanian, but only in a certain number of words, *ŭ* represents **ō;* **ā* is always represented by Lith. *o* and Lett. *ā*,
which correspond as well to some of the occurrences of IE.
*ō. In Indo-Iranian, Slavic, Old Prussian, and Germanic,
the fusion of *ā* and *ō* is complete, whence II. *ā*, Sl. *a*, OPruss.
ā, Germ. *ō*. The fusion of *ō* and *ā*, then, does not extend
quite as far as that of *ŏ* and *ă*, and that is natural since long
vowels are more stable than short vowels by the very fact of
their length; the fusion of *ō* and *ā*, however, takes place
only in areas where *ŏ* and *ă* fall together as well. Here again
is an example of the independence of isoglosses.

It remains to be seen whether the fusion of *o* and *a* is
of Indo-European origin in the languages indicated. This
is not clear. However, the continuity of the two areas is
such that the origin of the tendency toward fusion must
almost certainly have been Indo-European, and such that
the fusion itself was perhaps already completed at the
Indo-European stage (at least as far as the short vowels
are concerned).

As for Indo-Iranian, an objection will no doubt be raised
based on K. Brugmann's law, according to which **o* (alternating with **e*) is represented by *ā* in Indo-Iranian open
syllables. But this law, it seems, must in the end be rejected,
despite all attempts at correction.[1] Isolated examples such
as Skr. *dámaḥ* = Gr. δόμος, *kalá* (cf. Lith. *skalà* and *skeliù*),
divā-karáḥ (cf. *cárati*) evidently suffice to deny Brugmann's
hypothesis.

For Germanic, which is at the extremity of the area of
o– and *a–*fusion and in which, consequently, it would not
be surprising to find that the process had been completed
later than elsewhere, certain cases have been pointed out in
which **o* in an unstressed syllable supposedly survived

until the historical period. However, the unstressed *o* of proper nouns transcribed by foreigners, e.g., *Langobardi,* proves very little; nor is there any precise conclusion to be drawn from forms such as OHG. *tagum,* etc. In all these cases, there seems to have been some influence of the labials upon the unaccented vowels.[2] Even if these occurrences of *o* are original, they do not prove that there was no fusion of *a* and *o,* for the treatment of *a* in this position is unknown for want of examples.

In addition, it has been thought that *k^w* underwent delabialization in Germanic before an original *o,* while *$k^w a$* surely retained its labiovelar value. However, the examples of this delabialization before *o* are disputed and uncertain.[3] And even if this doubtful hypothesis is accepted, it is still not clearly demonstrated that the tendency for *o* and *a* to fall together postdates Indo-European and is really Germanic; since the labiovelars are of Indo-European date, delabialization before *o* could also be Indo-European, occurring in the dialect ultimately giving rise to Germanic.

The fusion of *o* and *a,* then, provides an isogloss that is both clearly drawn and distinct from the one marking the gutturals.

chapter seven

The Cluster *-tt-*

IN THOSE CASES IN WHICH A MORPHOLOGICAL element ends with a dental consonant and the following element begins with a *t,* the Indo-European languages show two different developments: *ss* in Italic, Celtic and Germanic, *st* in the other languages (including Albanian, Illyrian, Thracian, and Phrygian[1]). There are no sure examples in Armenian; the connection is questionable, for instance, between *xist* 'hard' and *xit* 'tight, pressed' or Skr. *khidáti* 'he tears, squeezes'. Sanskrit needs to be discussed all by itself. Examples: Av. *hastō,* in contrast to Lat. *-sessus,* Ir. *sess* 'seat'; Lith.-*èstas,* Gr. (ἄρι-) στον, in contrast to Lat. *ēsus,* OHG. *ās,* Ir. *ess.*

Here Italic, Celtic, and Germanic all present the same innovation; it is unexpected and consequently characteristic. The concordance among the other languages is less instructive, though noteworthy: Greek belongs here with the Eastern languages, and not with the Western group consisting of Italic, Celtic, and Germanic.

When the second morphological element in question begins with a voiced dental (or voiced aspirated dental), the result is *zd(h)* in the dialects having *st.* As for the Western dialects, no fact is clearly attested and the development is hard to determine; see below the discussion of Lat. *crēdō,* OIr. *cretim.* Example: GAv. *vōizdyāi* 'in order to know', Lith. *véizdi* 'see', Gr. $\digamma i\sigma\theta\iota$. In Iranian, under the conditions defined by Bartholomae's law, there is also *zd;* thus, Av. *baozdri* 'female animal learning to know the male', from the root **bheudh-* with the suffix **-ter-* in the feminine; Greek naturally shows $-\sigma\tau$-: $\pi\acute{v}\sigma\tau\iota\varsigma$.

There is a children's word which keeps *tt* (or simplifies it to *t*) in both dialect groups; in the Western group, it is Lat. *atta,* Ir. *aite* (*t* supposing *tt,* since *t* would have given *th* here), Goth. *atta,* OHG. *atto;* in the Eastern group, Gr. $\mathring{a}\tau\tau a$, Alb. *at,* Oss. *äda,* OSl. *otĭci.* The word offers some difficulty; to say that this special case is due to the fact that the word belongs to the speech of children resolves nothing, because children's language is, after all, transmitted by speakers who have reached their full linguistic development. In reality, the rules relating to the treatment of **tt* (or **ddh*) are rules of morphological gradation; these rules are no doubt based on a very early phonological change in Indo-European; but the rule of gradation in question did not apply to the double consonants of children's language, which consonants could, besides, have had a pronunciation different from that of the double consonants brought about by morphological combinations.

It may appear surprising that Sanskrit regularly shows *tt* where the other languages have either *st* or *ss,* as in *sattáḥ, vittáḥ, átti, véttha,* etc., or, with *ddh, viddhí, buddhíḥ, boddhar-,* etc. Close examination, however, reveals that Sanskrit once had, but then eliminated, a change of **tt* and **ddh* parallel to the change that is found in the other Eastern dialects.

This is very clear as far as the voiced cluster is concerned. Alongside the treatment attested in Skr. *viddhí, buddhíḥ,* we find, in fact, another, based on **-zdh-,* in the following four imperatives in *-dhi:*

(1) *dhehí* 'put', a form found in the Rig-Veda, in contrast to *dhattāt, dhattá, dhatsvá.*

(2) *dehí* 'give', found ten times in the Rig-Veda, whereas *daddhi* occurs there eight times; cf. Av. *dazdi.* The *d* was sometimes restored under the influence of *dattá, dadmasi, dádati.* Similar restoration did not take place in the case of *dhehí* because the forms *dadhmasi, dádhati,* having a medial *dh* and, consequently, an initial *d,* were further removed from *dhehí.* (The *dh* of *dhehí,* which is not phonetically correct, is attributable to the influence of the other forms of the root *dhā-;* it was generalized because it allowed for the differentiation of *dhehí* 'put' and *dehí* 'give'.)

(3) *bodhi* 'pay attention', an isolated athematic form in the Sanskrit root *budh-;* cf. nevertheless the 3rd-person plurals *ábudhram, ábudhran.*

(4) *yodhi* 'fight', found once in the Rig-Veda; cf. the participle *yodhānáḥ,* also athematic.

These four imperatives are the sole representatives of the phonological development **zdh* in Sanskrit; the other examples are at least doubtful. But wherever Skr. *-ddh-* appears, i.e., in almost all cases, it is to be explained by analogy. If we grant that the 2nd-person plural imperative *attá* is phonetically correct, we easily see how *addhí* could have been made over, as well as *viddhí, cikiddhí, mamaddhí;* and if the type *sattáḥ* is phonetically correct (cf. Av. *hastō*), the re-forming of the entire type *buddhíḥ, buddháḥ* is easily explained.

Sanskrit *çraddhá* 'faith', compared with Av. *zrazdā-,* is at first glance a problem. In Vedic, however, the first term of this juxtaposed compound could still occur in isolation, as in *çrát te dadhāmi;* this suffices to justify the form with *ddh.* Latin *crēdō* and OIr. *cretim* (in which *t* is simply the spelling for *d*) are one and the same word; yet the outcome of *-ddh-* in Latin and Irish cannot be deduced therefrom, since, at the time when the treatment of the double dental became fixed, both elements could still have been, and no doubt were, autonomous. Latin *crēdō* proves no more concerning the outcome of *-ddh-* in Latin than the 3rd-person *ēst* does concerning the treatment of *-tt-* (the phonetically correct form is provided by *ēsus*).

The word *addhá* 'truly' (cf. OPers. and GAv. *azdā*) is troublesome; if its formation were clear, and not obscure as it is, the solution would surely be apparent.

Johansson (*IF*, XIV, 310) has attempted to prove that the outcome of *-tt-* in Sanskrit is *-st-*, as in the other Eastern dialects. Except, perhaps, for one or two, the etymologies which he adduces do not give his theory any firm support; they are more or less doubtful, concerned for the most part with rare and poorly attested words. Now, any etymology which is not clear and convincing is devoid of interest; it is always possible to scatter around any theory a great number of somewhat plausible derivational relations. These relations become acceptable only if the theory is based on some certainties; if all of them are either wholly or largely wanting in obvious truth, then despite their apparent possibility they cannot prove anything and have no value whatever.

One fact is certain: Indo-Iranian did not receive *-st-* and *-zdh-*. It is known that *s* and *z* always become *š* and *ž* after *i*, *u*, and *r* in Indo-Iranian. Now, in Iranian, *-itt-*, *-utt-*, and *-rtt-* result in *-ist-*, *-ust-*, and *-rst-*, as in Av. *vistō*, *-kərəstō*, etc. The same observation holds for *-ddh-*, for Vedic has *bodhi*, *yodhi*, and not **boḍhi*, **yoḍhi*, and Avestan has *baozdri*. Indo-Iranian, therefore, received *-tˢt-* and *-dᶻdh-*.

In Sanskrit, a sibilant between two stops falls: in con-

trast to *ábhakṣi,* there is *ábhakta* (cf. GAv. *bāxštā*); in contrast to *áchān, áchāntsuḥ,* there is *áchāntta;* and **ut-sthitaḥ*
results in *utthitáḥ.* Given that, the *tt* of Skr. *úttaraḥ* (= Gr.
ὕστερος) may represent **tˢt;* and, since in any case the
stage **st* was not yet reached when *i, u,* and *r* came to influence a following *s,* it is indeed **tˢt* that must be posited
as the Indo-Iranian form. And the historically attested
result of this **tˢt,* viz., *tt,* is precisely what is to be expected
in Sanskrit.

The fact that the normal development of **-dᶻdh-* was Skr.
*-zdh- (whence *dhehí, dehí, bodhi, yodhi*) is not an objection:
the voiced stop *d* has a less intense articulation than the
voiceless stop *t,* and **dᶻdh* can have become **zdh* without
necessarily entailing a shift from **tˢt* to **st.*

Johansson's conclusion, then, can hardly be accepted a
priori. Indeed, it must be rejected, for if we accept the
idea that original **tˢt* is reflected phonologically by Skr.
st, we do not see why such a development would have been
eliminated by analogy. All of the other languages preserved the development *-st-,* or even the stranger and
obscure development *-ss-;* could Sanskrit alone have entirely eliminated the type in all cases where it is so well
preserved everywhere else? Given the 2nd-person plural
attá 'eat', it is readily seen how the singular form *addhí* 'eat'
could be created by analogy, but no analogy compelled the
substitution of *attá* for an original **astá.* Even where the
flectional system brought about certain innovations, as in
Latin, the form *-tt-* was not restored (although the language had certain occurrences of *tt,* e.g., *atta, attingō,* etc.)
and what we find is *ēst, ēstis.* (Vollmer [*Glotta,* I, 113] questions the value of the grammarians' statements on which
the assertion of the long quantity in *ēst, ēstis* is based.)

Only one of Johansson's examples can cause any serious
doubt: Skr. *ásthi* (gen. *asthnáḥ*) 'bone', beside Av. *ast-,*
Pers. *ast,* Gr. *ὀστέον,* Arm. *oskr* (from **ost-w-er-?*) and Lat.
os (*ossis*) and *ossu, ossum* (the word is not attested in the

other languages with the development -ss-). By starting
with *ot^{s}th-, we could explain the Latin form, which is
otherwise very obscure, and, furthermore, Skr. *ásthi* certainly represents normal phonological development. However, since Johansson's hypothesis must be rejected for the
reasons already indicated, Lat. *os* must be explained in
another way: just as we find in Slavic the -es–stem *oko*,
očese (cf. Skr. *ákṣi*) together with the stem with zero-suffix
ok- in the dual *oči*, we may posit *osth-s-* to explain Lat. *oss-*
(as Johansson himself once did).

In conclusion, then, the Indo-Iranian outcome of *-tt-*,
-ddh- is *-t^{s}t-*, *-d^{z}dh-;* and it is no doubt upon the same
original forms that the other Eastern dialects base their
-st-, -zdh-. In contrast to this development, Italic, Celtic
and Germanic have -ss-.

chapter eight

The Development of *ə

ALL INDO-EUROPEAN DIALECTS HAVE ă (OR Sl. *o*, representing *ă) for the Indo-European sound *ə. Only Indo-Iranian differs, having *i* (Skr. *pitá*, Av. *pita*, in contrast to Gr. πατήρ, Lat. *pater*, OIr. *athir*, Goth. *fadar*, Arm. *hayr*). Greek, moreover, has ε or o in those cases where *ə alternates with ē or ō, as in τίθημι, τίθεμεν; γνητός, γενετήρ; δίδωμι, δίδομεν, etc., and this deviation shows that the timbre of *ə was still ill defined at the time when the Hellenic development became fixed.

The weakness of *ə, a quite special sound whose singularity has been brilliantly established by Saussure in his *Mémoire sur le système primitif des voyelles dans les langues indo-européennes* (Leipzig, 1879), stems from various circumstances, principally the following:

(1) The element *ə not only never survives before a vowel, but disappears without leaving any trace; thus, Skr. *ján-aḥ*, Gr. γέν-ος, Lat. *gen-us*, in contrast to Skr. *jani-tă*, Gr. γενε-τήρ, Lat. *geni-tor*. A form such as διδόασι is a

peculiarly Greek innovation, and it is the type Ved. *d-úh̥* 'they gave', *dád-ati* 'they give' which represents the Indo-European situation.

(2) The element $*\partial$ combines with a preceding sonant if the sonant itself is not preceded by a vowel; this gives rise to the so-called long sonants, viz., $*\bar{u}$ and $*\bar{i}$ on the one hand, and $*\bar{\underset{\circ}{n}}$, $*\bar{\underset{\circ}{m}}$, $*\bar{\underset{\circ}{r}}$, and $*\bar{\underset{\circ}{l}}$ on the other. Examples:

Skr. *pū-táh̥*, Lat. *pū-rus*, OIr. *ū-nad* 'purification', in contrast to Skr. *pavi-tram* 'means of purification'.

Skr. *jā-táh̥*, Lat. *(g)nātus*, Gaul. *-gnātos*, in contrast to Skr. *janitā́*, etc.

Skr. *pūrṇáh̥*, OIr. *lā-n*, Lith. *pìl-nas*, OSl. *plŭ-nŭ* (Serb. *pȕn*), in contrast to Ved. *pári-man-*.

The exact nature of $*\bar{\underset{\circ}{n}}$, $*\bar{\underset{\circ}{m}}$, $*\bar{\underset{\circ}{r}}$, $*\bar{\underset{\circ}{l}}$ in Indo-European does not matter here; the essential fact is that $*\partial$ often combines with a preceding sonant.

These two features of $*\partial$ are Common Indo-European. A third feature, however, also attesting the weakness of $*\partial$, is dialectal in character:

In medial position, i.e., in a syllable that is neither initial nor final, $*\partial$ generally remains in Sanskrit on the one hand and in Greek, Italic, and Celtic on the other, but it always falls in Iranian, Slavic, Baltic, Armenian, and Germanic. The survival of $*\partial$ in Sanskrit does not attest any special relation of Sanskrit with Greek, Italic, and Celtic, for this is nothing more than a matter of preservation of the original situation. However, the common fall of $*\partial$ in geographically connected languages (Iranian, Slavic, Baltic, Armenian, and Germanic) is to be noted as an important dialectal phenomenon.

The characteristic example is Skr. *duhitā́*, Gr. θυγάτηρ, but GAv. *dug∂dā* (dissyllabic), Av. *duγδa*, Arm. *dustr*, OSl. *dŭšti*, Lith. *duktē̃*, Goth. *dauhtar*. The fall of $*\partial$ came early enough for Bartholomae's law to have been applied in

Indo-Iranian; Persian nevertheless has *duxt, duxtar;* but
the voiceless consonant can be explained by an influence
of the *t* in **mātar-, *pitar-, *brātar-* on the original Old
Persian form of Pers. *duxt, duxtar.*

In Slavic and Baltic,**ə* falls in medial position without
leaving any apparent trace after a stop, as in Sl. *męsti*
'disturb', in contrast to Ved. *mánthitavaí;* Lith. *spleczù,*
splĕsti and *splintù, splìsti* or *plantù, plàsti,* and OSl. *plesna*
'sole (of the foot)' (from **plethəsnā*), in contrast to Skr.
prathi-mán-, pr̥thi-ví, Gr. πλατα-μών, Πλατα-ιαί, πλάτα-νος,
Gaul. *Lita-via,* OIr. *letha-n* 'broad'.

In Lithuanian and Slavic, as Saussure has shown, the fall
of **ə* after a sonant brought about the acute intonation of
the new diphthong thus produced, in opposition to the
circumflex intonation of the original diphthongs; thus, IE.
*ert gives Lith. *er̃t,* Russ. *éret,* Serb. *rìjet,* but **erət* gives Lith.
ért, Russ. *erêt,* Serb. *r̃ĕt.* In contrast to Lat. *moli-tus,* for
example, we find Lith. *málti* 'grind, mill', Russ. *molót',*
Serb. *mljĕti.* Similarly, the long sonants **n̥̄, *m̥̄, *r̥̄, *l̥̄,* which
are composed of **n, *m, *r, *l* plus **ə,* give Baltic and Slavic
acute diphthongs, in contrast with the short sonants **n̥,*
*m̥, *r̥, *l̥; thus, we find Lith. *pìlnas,* Serb. *pùn* alongside
Skr. *pūrṇáḥ,* OIr. *lān,* but Lith. *vìlkas,* Serb. *vûk* alongside
Skr. *vr̥̂kaḥ.* The fall of **ə,* then, has certain very definite
effects in Baltic and Slavic.

In Germanic, there are no examples of the preservation
of medial **ə,* and there are examples in which the fall of **ə*
is certain; thus, OSax. *kind* from **genə-tó-;* in contrast to
Gr. πετά-ννῡμι, πέτα-λον, we have OHG. *fedel(-gold)* and
OE. *(gold-)fell* 'gold-leaf' (**féþla-* and **feðlá-*) and OE.
fæðm, OSax. *fathmos* 'both arms outstretched'. A form
such as OIce. *sörum* 'we sowed' is explained, then, by the
influence of *sörun,* in which *-un* represents **-n̥t;* it is not
based directly on **sesəmó,* as has sometimes been thought.
In final syllable, it seems that **ə* gave *u;* the *u* of OHG.

anut, in contrast to Lat. *anas* (*anitis*) and Lith. *ántis,* comes from the nominative singular. In contrast to Lith. *mélžu* 'I milk' from **meləg-,* the nominative singular also furnishes Goth. *miluks* 'milk', OHG. *miluh,* OAS. *meoluc,* OIce. *mi̯olk;* the form of the other cases is preserved in OE. *milc.*[1] The fall of **ə* was no doubt followed by a diphthongal form, different at first from the original form, as in Baltic and Slavic; but most Germanic dialects eliminated this feature. Nevertheless, Old High German still shows some traces of it, e.g., OHG. *halam,* alongside OIce. *halmr* (cf. Serb. *slȁma,* Russ. *solóma,* Gr. κάλαμος); OHG. *birihha,* alongside OE. *beorc* (cf. Lith. *béržas,* Serb. *brèza,* Russ. *berëza*). In these examples, the *a* of *halam* and the *i* of *birihha* are not directly representative of **ə,* but a kind of resonance stemming from the special pronunciation of the diphthong produced by the fall of **ə.*

Armenian offers no decisive example except *dustr.* We might additionally cite *geṫmn* 'fleece', which belongs to the family of Skr. *ū́rṇā,* Serb. *vȕna,* Lith. *vìlna,* Lat. *lāna,* and then posit the form **welə-;* Lat. *vellus* was influenced by the verb *vellō.* There is no contrary example, however, for the *a* of *ara-wr* 'plough' may correspond to the *ā* of Lat. *arātrum,* *arā-re* as well as to the **ə* of Gr. ἄροτρον, Lith. *árklas,* Serb. *rȁlo.* Let us note, too, Arm. *armukn* 'elbow', cf. Skr. *īrmáḥ* and Serb. *rȁme;* there is no way of determining whether Arm. *ar-* is based here on **r̥̄-* or **arə-,* but in either case **ə* is not represented; Arm. *ar* is the outcome of short **r̥,* and the developments of **r̥* and **r̥̄* merge only in those languages which, like Germanic, lost medial **ə:* Goth. *fulls* 'full' from **fulnaz* presupposes **pl̥(ə)nos,* with the fall of **ə.* Likewise, it is unknown whether, in Arm. *(dr-)and-kh* 'door post', *an* is based on **anə* (cf. Lat. *antae* [from **anətā-,* with syncope of medial *a*]) or on **n̥* (cf. Skr. *átāḥ*); even in the latter case, **ə* fell, for Arm. *an* is the outcome of short **n̥.*

As for Iranian, the regularity of the fall of medial **ə*

has been challenged.[2] The examples of fall of *ə are clear
and beyond question: Skr. *brávīti*, Av. *mraoiti;* Skr. *dráviṇaḥ*,
Av. *draonō;* Skr. *tamisra-*, Av. *tąθra-* (Pers. *tār*), etc. The
contrary examples, on the other hand, are worthless. There
are aorists in *-iš-*, but the *i* is to be explained by an original
-i-, like the *i* of Lat. *-līqu-is-tī*. In OPers. *hadiš* and Av.
hadiš, the *i* representing *ə (or rather, *i*) is in final syllable.
The occurrences of Av. *airime* 'calmly', unlike the com-
pound-initial form *armaē-*, are all in prose texts, and in no
passage can it be stated with certainty that the word has
three syllables. It is true that *ə falls occasionally, even in
initial syllable, e.g., GAv. *ptā, ptarəm, fδrōi*, in contrast to Av.
pita; however, this fall can be explained by the ancient
occurrence of juxtaposed compounds such as Ved. *dyaúṣ
pitá* (cf. Lat. *Iuppiter*). It is also true that medial *ə is sometimes not represented in Sanskrit, as in *dadmasi, dadmahe;*
however, analogy with the 3rd-person plural *dád-ati*, in
which *ə is correctly wanting before a vowel, suffices to
explain these forms. And *i* is not wanting in Sanskrit
wherever some such analogy would not explain its elimination. The presence or absence of accent never has any
connection with the fall of *ə.

The fall of medial *ə is common to Iranian, Slavic,
Baltic, Armenian, and Germanic. Certain curious contrasts
result, such as that of Russ. *terét'*, Cz. *třiti*, and Gr. *τέρε-τρον*,
Lat. *tere-bra*, Ir. *tara-thar* (from *t°rə-*), Wel. *taradr;* or OIce.
ǫnd 'breath', *anda* 'breathe, blow', but Skr. *ániti* 'he breathes,
blows', *áni-laḥ* 'wind', Gr. *άνε-μος*, Lat. *ani-ma*, Ir. *ana-l*,
Wel. *ana-dl*.

The contraction of the sonant *y and a following *ə, resulting in *ī, is no doubt a phenomenon of Common Indo-
European antedating the dialectal fall of medial *ə. The
zero-grade form *-ī- of the athematic optative suffix is
attested in Iranian (GAv. *vairīmaidī*), Slavic (OSl. *dadimŭ*,
dadite) and Germanic (Goth. *gebeima*, OHG. *wurtīmēs*); it is

unlikely that the *ī* of these optatives would stem from analogy with forms with the vowel in final syllable, for in Indo-European time the 2nd-person singular active was **-yēs* and the 3rd **-yēt*, with *e*–grade.

To appreciate what the coincidence of these languages means, we must note that **ə* sometimes falls in other Indo-European dialects as well, but under different conditions.

In Sanskrit, medial **ə* (but not final **-ə*) always fell after *y* preceded by a vowel, giving rise to the Sanskrit diphthong *e*,[3] as in the following examples:

Skr. *bibhéti* 'he fears'; cf. Lith. *báimè* and Skr. *bhītáḥ*, Lett. *bītēs*, in which *ī* indicates the dissyllabic character of the root.

Skr. *kreṣyati* 'he will buy'; cf. Gr. *ἐ-πριά-μην* and Skr. *krītáḥ* (with *ī*).

Skr. *adīdet* 'it shone'; cf. Hom. *δέα-το* and Skr. *didīhí*, *-dītiḥ* (with *ī*).

Skr. *rétaḥ* 'running, current', alongside *riṇáti, rītíḥ;* whether the connection is with Lat. *rīvus* or with Lith. *léti* and *lýti*, the origin is still IE. **eyə.*

Skr. *nétar-* and *netár-* 'leader', aorist subjunctive *neṣati*, in contrast to *nītáḥ.*

Skr. *-kṣetoḥ* 'destroy', alongside *kṣīṇa-* and *kṣiṇáti.*

Skr. *-metoḥ* 'damage', *meṣṭa*, alongside *mīta-* and *mináti.*

Skr. *pretár-, premán-*, in contrast to *prītáḥ* and *prīṇáti;* cf. OSl. *prijati* and Goth. *frijon.*

Skr. *ápīpet, péruḥ*, in contrast to *pīnáḥ* and *pyáyate;* cf. also Lith. *pénas* 'milk'.

Skr. *adīdhet* 'he thought'; cf. *dhītáḥ* and *dhyāti.*

Skr. *véti* 'he pursues'; cf. Gr. *ϝίεμαι*, Lith. *vejù, výti* and Skr. *vītíḥ*, OSl. *(vŭz-)viti* 'gain'.

Skr. *jihreti* 'he is ashamed'; cf. *hrītáḥ.*

Sanskrit, then, has *e* where *aya* would be expected. If the outcome of **ə* after *y* were *i*, we might understand a contraction of **ayi;* but the 1st person *-ya* of the middle optative, in contrast to the ordinary secondary ending *-i* of the 1st-person middle, shows that **ə* is represented in Sanskrit by *a* after *y* as well as before *y*. Wherever Sanskrit shows *ayi* within a word, we have to do with a secondary form, created by analogy. Thus Vedic has dissyllabic *jétar-;*[4] later, we find *jayitar-;* however, the verbal adjective *jitáḥ*, with its *ĭ*, is sufficient to indicate the secondary nature of *jayitar-*, which, besides, is of later attestation than *jétar-*.

Nevertheless, a trace of the fall of **ə* in Sanskrit is sometimes seen in the dissyllabic value of the diphthong *e* representing **eyə;* we thus have trisyllabic *netár-* and *pretár-*, as has been noted by J. Wackernagel;[5] even so, we must not reconstruct **nayitár-*, **prayitár-*, which are purely imaginary forms.[6]

Since at the end of a word the sometimes dissyllabic *ā* of Indo-Iranian (for example, in the genitive plural in *-ām*) corresponds to a long vowel with circumflex intonation in Lithuanian, the sometimes dissyllabic Sanskrit diphthong *e* (II. *ai*) in medial position would correspond, if the situation arose, to a diphthong with acute intonation in Lithuanian. There is nothing surprising about that; in each language the development of intonational patterns took place independently, and under conditions that varied from one language to another; Baltic and Slavic intonational patterns stem from Indo-European phenomena of various kinds, and the grouping is purely Baltic and Slavic.

In Greek, as Saussure[7] has briefly indicated, IE. **ə* falls after a syllable with *o*–vocalism, as in the following examples:

τόρμος 'hole': τέρετρον.

ὅλμος 'mortar' (from **olə-smos?*): ἀλέω. (Bartholomae has connected this with Skr. *sūrmí*, a connection which, though changing the etymology, would allow our example to remain; the origin would then be **solə-mos* or **solə-smos*.[8])

πόρνη 'harlot, (Lat.) meretrix': ἐπέρασσα, πιπράσκω.

πότμος 'lot, fate': πεσοῦμαι (from *πετε-ομαι), πέπτωκα.

τόλμα: τελαμών, τλᾱ-, ταλα-.

βροντή: -βρεμέτης.

κόρση: κέρας (and likewise in the other cases in which the development ορ from IE. *r̥ has been posited[9]).

πορθμός (cf. OHG. *farm*): περάω, πέρας.

οἶσος: ϝιτέα; cf. Lith. *výti*, Lat. *viēre*.

φόρτος 'burden', φορμός 'basket': φέρετρον and φαρέτρᾱ, Lesb. φερένᾱ, -φρήσω. The noun forms of the root are generally dissyllabic in Greek; cf. moreover Skr. *bharítram* and Lat. *(prae-)fericulum*, Skr. *bhárīman-*, Lat. *(of-)ferumenta*, Russ. *berémja*, Serb. *br̃eme*, Cz. *br̃ímĕ*. Nevertheless, the root also has monosyllabic forms, especially Gr. φέρμα. It has been noted that φέρτρον is found even in Homer, and Attic has φερνή, beside Lesb. φερένᾱ; it is true that φερνή could be considered a contamination of *φορνᾱ and φερενᾱ. It is still curious that there should be no dissyllabic form with *o* in the first syllable; instead, we find only φόρτος and φορμός.

μορφή may be connected with Lith. *márgas,* as suggested by Solmsen (*KZ*, XXXIV, 23); the gloss ἀμερφές· αἰσχρόν (Hes.) would have been influenced by μορφή, an inevitable occurrence because of the series of short vowels brought about by the form *ἀμεραφες.

δοάσσατο, then, owes its α to the influence of δέατο, and στοναχή stems from στενάχω.

The ι of Gr. δολιχός is unexplained: the ε of ἐνδελεχής corresponds to the expected IE. *ə; cf., with different root vocalism, Skr. *dīrghắḥ*, Av. *darəγō*, OSl. *dlĭgŭ* (Serb. *dȕg*), Lith. *ìlgas* and, on the other hand, Ved. *drāghmán-* and Av. *drājō* 'length'. As obscure as the ι of δολιχός may be, it is at least striking that this form with its *o*–vocalism does not contain one of the normal developments of IE. *ə, like the ε in ἐνδελεχής which is comparable to the ε in τίθεμεν. (The form *δληχ-which the ε of -δελεχης presupposes is not attested.)

The same fall of *ə after o–vocalism apparently took place in Latin too, as shown by the following examples:

Lat. *culmus;* cf. Russ. *solóma,* Serb. *slàma,* Cz. *sláma;* and, after zero-grade vocalism, Gr. κάλαμος (from *$k_1$oləmos*).

Lat. *collis;* cf. Lith. *kálnas* 'mountain'.

Lat. *spūma* (cf. OHG. *feim,* OE. *fām*); cf. Lith. *spáinė,* Serb. *pjèna,* Russ. *p'éna,* Cz. *pina.*

Lat. *forda;* cf., with *e*–grade, Russ. *berëžaja,* Serb. *brèda* (a doubtful example, because of the double form of the root: *bher-* and *bherə-*).

It seems hard to find a Celtic example in any way probative. Sanskrit *badhiráḥ* 'deaf, muffled' and OIr. *bodar,* Wel. *byddar* are ambiguous, for Skr. *-ira-* and Celt. *-aro-* may represent *-ºro-* and *-əro-;* and, if OIr. *tarann* 'thunder', Wel. *tarann* are to be seen as cognates of Lith. *tarti* 'say' (formerly 'make noise'—a frequent change of meaning), Lithuanian intonation shows that Celt. *-an-* here represents *-ºn-,* and not *-ən-.*

There is nothing that can be said about Sanskrit, which combined *e* and *o* in the single sound *a.* It is curious that there is a Vedic vocative *omāsaḥ* alongside *avitā* 'protector', with the plural form *ūmāḥ.* But certainly no doctrine could be founded upon such an isolated example.

As we have seen, medial *ə tended to become mute throughout the Indo-European family. The fall of *ə was accomplished under identical conditions in Iranian, Slavic, Baltic, Armenian, and Germanic on the one hand and, on the other hand, in Greek and Latin (and perhaps elsewhere; examples are wanting). Sanskrit shows a type of fall after *y* that is unique; similarly, Indo-Iranian shows a unique development of *i* from IE. *ə.

chapter nine

The Cluster *-wy-*

IN MEDIAL POSITION, THE SONANT CLUSTER *-wy-* shows two different developments. If we take as our type the case in which the cluster is followed by the vowel *o*, we find *-owyo-* in Sanskrit, Armenian, Greek, Italic, and Celtic, but *-ouyo-* in Iranian, Slavic, Letto-Lithuanian, Gothic, and Scandinavian — i.e., Skr. *-avya-*, Gr. -οιο- (from *-ογγο-*), Lat. *-ovio-*, Gaul. *-ovio-*, but Av. *-aoya-*, Sl. *-uje-*, Lith. *-auja-*, Goth. *-auja-*, as in the following examples:

Skr. *návyah*, Ion. νεîος, Lat. *Novius*, Gaul. *Novio(-dūnum)*, Wel. *newydd*, Ir. *nūe* (assuming *nowyos*), but Lith. *naŭjas*, Goth. *niujis*.

Skr. *savyáh* 'left', but Av. *haoyō*, Pahl. *hōy, hōyak* (the Avestan spelling is therefore correct), OSl. *šuji* (from *seuyos* giving *sjeujos*).

Skr. *gávyah* and *gavyáh* 'bovine', Arm. *kogi* 'butter', Gr. (ἐννεά-)βοιος, but Av. *gaoyam* 'bovine' (fem. accus.).

In Gothic, the flectional system reveals the existence of this phonetic principle in the contrast between nominative *hawi* 'grass' and genitive *haujis,* dative *hauja.*

The force of analogy sometimes interferes with the action of the law. Thus, Lithuanian has the 1st-person form *aviù* 'I wear . . . on my feet' by analogy with *avéti* and the rest of the present flection, with *i*-suffix, e.g., 3rd person *āvi;* with the suffix *-*ye*-, Slavic has the phonetically correct form *ob-ujǫ.* Moreover, with this suffix *-*ye*-, the diphthong is normal in Baltic and Slavic, as in OSl. *pljujǫ,* Lith. *spiáuju* 'I spit' and so on in all other examples.

Adjectives in *-*yo*- (*-*yā*-) derived from -*u*–stems have the phonetically correct form in Sanskrit and Avestan, e.g., Skr. -*avya*-, Av. -*aoya*-. Old Slavic *synovljĭ* 'of the son' stems from analogy with *synovi* (dat. sg.), *synove* (nom. pl.), etc. The phonetically correct type is provided by *ujĭ* 'maternal grandfather'; OPruss. *awis* (same meaning) owes its form to the fact that the nominative singular occurs with -*is* in Baltic. After a long vowel or diphthong, this development is normal, as in Av. *daēvya*- from *daēva*- 'demon'; or OSl. *stavljǫ* (1st pers.), which is close to 2nd person *staviši* and the infinitive *staviti* 'stand [something] up'.

If, as H. Pedersen believes (*KZ*, XXXVIII, 196), IE. *-*w*- gives Arm. *g* in intervocalic position, we could interpret Arm. *kogi* 'butter' as stemming from East IE. *gowiyo-, and the example would not be probative for the Armenian outcome of *-*owyo*-. It is even necessary to start with *-*ogiyo*- to explain a genitive such as *kogwoy* 'of the butter', but the *i* may be due to a re-formation on analogy with the nominative-accusative *kogi*. It is difficult to find an example to refute Pedersen's theory, because the structure of Armenian entails a final *w* (or *v*) in the nominative and accusative singular of the nouns supplying the examples, and this

form suffices to explain all the others which might otherwise serve to refute Pedersen; thus, *tewem* 'I last' runs
counter to Pedersen's theory, but the form *tew* 'duration'
accounts for it, and so on with all the other examples.
However, if Pedersen's theory is not refutable, it is not
demonstrable either, for the genitive *aregi* of *arew* may
be explained by **rewy^e/_os* just as *kogi* may be explained
by **gowyo-*. Similarly, *taygr* 'husband's brother' may be
based on **daiwr-* (cf. the genitive-dative *hawr* = Gr. $\pi\alpha\tau\rho\acute{o}\varsigma$,
$\pi\alpha\tau\rho\acute{\iota}$), and nothing proves that **w* became *g* in intervocalic
position. It is hard to see why intervocalic **w* should have
become *g:* the shift from initial **w* to *g*, which is not even
regular in Armenian, is due to initial glide; in Persian,
where **w* is represented either by *b* or by *g* in initial position, the same treatment does not recur in intervocalic
position. The Armenian word *aregakn* 'sun', which Pedersen cites as his authority, is of uncertain interpretation.[1]
The supposed law necessitates giving up the attractive
interpretation of Arm. *howiw* 'shepherd' as arising from
*owi-pā-, and undermines the otherwise very satisfying
connection of Arm. *govem* 'I praise' to OSl. *govĕti* 'take
care of'.

In the case of Germanic, K. Brugmann (*Grundriss*, I,
797) maintains that West Germanic keeps **-wy-;* according
to him, OHG. and OSax. *niuwi*, OE. *nēowe, nīwe* have **-wy-*
with the consonant-doubling typical of West Germanic
before -*y*-. However, there is no less reason to suppose an
original **neu^wyo-*, for the diphthong of Goth. *niujis* is
clearly evident there. The West Germanic form is in-
teresting in that it exhibits some trace of consonantal *w*
before *y* while at the same time containing the diphthong.

No doubt this same point of departure must be posited
for Common Baltic. Indeed, while the Old Prussian
Vocabulary of Elbing has *crauys,* alongside Lith. *kraũjas*

'blood' (cf. Skr. *kravyam*), the Encheiridion has *krawia*, *krawian*, as has been shown by Zupitza (*KZ*, XL, 252); and the verbal forms include the 3rd person *-awie* (ibid., and see Bezzenberger, *KZ*, XLI, 85). Zupitza has even concluded from the Lithuanian form *naũjas* (and not **niaujas*) that the pronunciation *au* postdates the shift from **ew* to *av* in Lithuanian; there could, however, have been dissimilatory loss of the *j* caused by the medial *j*. The Old Prussian phenomenon survives and concurs with West Germanic in affirming the intermediary phase **-euʷye-*, which must be posited for Iranian, Slavic, Baltic, and Germanic. What we have here is a trace of the double pronunciation of consonants before a sonant that is presupposed by the long quantity of the first syllable in clusters such as *etre, etwe* and *esye* in Indo-European; this pronunciation is, moreover, attested directly in Sanskrit by the grammarians.[2] There arose, for this cluster, a quite serious difficulty, one that the various dialects resolved in different ways.

In those cases where *w* is doubled, the first element of the double articulation normally has the appearance of the *u* which occurs in the second half of a diphthong. Thus, in Homer there are old forms, no doubt Aeolian, such as ἀϝίαχος equivalent to ἀ(ϝ)ίαχος (*Il.* XIII, 41), εὔαδεν equivalent to ἔ(ϝ)αδεν (*Il.* XIV, 340), etc.; the initial ϝ is doubled here, as are λ, μ, ν and ρ in many analogous examples, but the double ϝ is written υ(ϝ), and not ϝϝ. In Cyprus, the Idalion Tablet bears the phrase *e u ve re ta sa tu* (εὐϝρητασατυ), with *e ve re ta sa tu* (ἐϝρητασατυ) a few lines below. When doubling occurs at the beginning of a word, this notation, which would disfigure the preceding word, is not used — whence, for example, ἀπὸ '(ϝϝ)έο (*Il.* XIII, 163). Thus we can explain the pronunciation **-auʷye-*. Nevertheless, this solution gives too much importance to the first element of the cluster, which was a double sonant, but surely a weak one. The first part of the double element was no doubt quite short; this relative brevity kept it distinct from the *u* that occurs as the second element in an ordinary *u*–diphthong in a sizable portion of the area of Indo-European, where the outcome thus appears to have been *-*owye-*.[3]

chapter ten

The Voiced Aspirated Stops

WHAT WE MEAN BY VOICED ASPIRATED STOPS is the group of sounds defined by the following series of correspondences:

In Sanskrit, voiced stops accompanied by a glottal articulation transcribed as *h*.

In Iranian, Slavic, Baltic, Albanian, and Celtic, voiced stops that have merged with the original pure (i.e., unaspirated) voiced stops—so that, for example, Iran. *d* = Skr. *d* and *dh*.

Germanic and Armenian also have voiced stops; these, however, are distinct from the original pure voiced stops, since the latter are now unvoiced. Otherwise, all these languages are alike in showing *d*, for example, as the equivalent of Skr. *dh*. F. Kluge[1] has seen the development of *ƀ*, *đ* and *γ* from the voiced aspirated stops as, perhaps, an Indo-European dialectal phenomenon, but this development is attested nowhere as a general development of the voiced aspirated stops; it is not attested for Germanic (see below, chap. XIII) or for any other Indo-European language. The spirant development appears everywhere as a weakening peculiar to certain positions, especially intervocalic.

Only Greek and Italic diverge, and they diverge in the same way, showing voiceless obstruents where all the other languages have voiced obstruents. In Greek, the voiceless aspirated stops of the ancient language — φ, θ, χ — became spirants in the course of historical development; the notations πh, κh are still found in old inscriptions. In Italic, from the very beginning of the written tradition and in every dialect, there are only spirants, and these spirants are already considerably modified: they are in part replaced by aspiration, h, and f is everywhere substituted for *þ. The very advanced Italic spirants almost certainly take the place of older voiceless aspirated stops like those attested in Greek. The similarity of Greek and Italic is striking, for no feature of the other early attested languages leads us to anticipate such a development.

If Macedonian is a Hellenic dialect (and if it is, it is a highly aberrant one), as O. Hoffmann — *Die Makedonen, ihre Sprache und ihr Volkstum* (Göttingen, 1906) — maintains, there might be some temptation to see in that fact an implicit argument against the Indo-European antiquity of voiceless articulation in Greek, since one of the most certain characteristic features of Macedonian is that it shows voiced stops where Greek has voiceless aspirated stops, as in δωραξ corresponding to θώραξ, ἀβρονϝες corresponding to ὀφρύες, etc. However, as Hoffmann notes, (p. 32), the voiceless aspirated stops are quite close to the voiced stops because of the weakness of their articulation. Moreover, by passing through a stage of spirant pronunciation, voiceless aspirated sounds may voice; thus, Germ. þ is represented by d in German, and certain Bantu dialects present analogous occurrences.[2]

If Italic and Greek belonged to wholly separate groups,

their similarity here would be considered fortuitous: voiced aspirated stops are represented by voiceless aspirated stops in Romany, as indicated by K. Brugmann (*Internationale Zeitschrift für allgemeine Sprachwissenschaft,* I, 226) and P. Kretschmer (*Einleitung,* p. 155). But Kretschmer is wrong to point to the shift from Gr. οὐδ'εἲς (grouped into one word, distinct from οὐδ' εἶς) to οὐθείς in order to establish that the tendency to unvoice voiced aspirated stops is recent in Greek and that it continued into the historical period; for δ followed by a rough breathing is something very different from the original voiced aspirated stops. Since, in addition, Greek and Italic belong to the same dialect groups from various points of view and share certain features not found outside Greek and Italic (see below, chap. XIX), it is not impossible that their resemblance in the present case may go back as far as the Indo-European stage; no definitive statement can be made.

(Add.) The unvoicing of voiced aspirated stops is the most striking feature supporting the affirmation of a special link between Greek and Italic. To be sure, the result differs considerably from one group to the other: in Greek, *bh, dh,* and *gh* gave *ph, th,* and *kh,* and it is only in the course of the historical period that the voiceless aspirated stops *ph, th,* and *kh* became spirants, at least in Ionic-Attic. And all the Italic dialects show only *f* and *h* in place of the original voiced aspirated stops in those instances where special conditions did not effect a return to voicedness. However, while the Italic development was more rapid than the Hellenic, passage through a voiceless-stop stage is likely to have occurred in both cases.

What casts doubt on the connection of the Greek and Italic developments is the fact that Celtic shows no participation. Now, on the one hand, Italo–Celtic unity is not uncertain. On the other hand, the distinction between aspirated and pure voiced stops, lost in Celtic in the historical period, still existed in ancient Celtic, since $*g^wh$ and $*gh$ combined to give g, while $*g^w$, which resulted in b, remained distinct from $*g$, which resulted in g. In the Italo–Celtic period, then, there was still a clear distinction between aspirated and unaspirated voiced stops, and the evolution of the aspirated series toward b, d, g on the one hand and toward f, h on the other, postdates the end of Italo–Celtic unity.

Whatever may have been the exact nature—heretofore ill defined—of the element distinguishing the voiced aspirated stops from the unaspirated type, it is easy to see that when Indo-European tongues were brought to Mediterranean peoples unfamiliar with voiced aspirated stops, this element brought about the process of unvoicing.

Indeed, the early voiced aspirated stops, which gave ancient Armenian the sounds transcribed as b, d, g, j and which are represented fairly completely in the East Armenian dialects by voiced stops, developed, in the West Armenian dialects, into voiceless stops, in part aspirated. The Eastern pronunciation of b, d, g preserves, at least in part, a sort of appendage that H. Adjarian has pointed out but has been unable to define precisely.[3] Father Rousselot has not been able to confirm the existence of this appendage,[4] but the appendage may still exist in some form that further phonetic experimentation could reveal. To explain how, in the Armenian dialects that have b, d, g from classical Armenian p, t, k, the b, d, and g of classical Armenian come to be represented by p, t, and k (or ph, th, kh), the most natural thing is to allow that Common Armenian b, d, g had some special feature comparable to that characterizing the Indo-European voiced aspirated stops. The resultant ph, th, and kh, observed by Adjarian, confirm the aspiration of the early voiced stops, which are written as letters corresponding to our b, d, g.[5]

Consequently, we may say that the unvoicing found in both Greek and Italic probably stems, first, from the preservation of the true character of the Indo-European voiced aspirated stops until the time of the arrival of Indo-European peoples — Hellenic on the one hand and Italo-Celtic on the other — in the Mediterranean basin, and secondly, from the fact that these sounds, encountering similar developmental conditions, evolved both independently and along parallel lines. There is, it would seem, no reason to refer to this matter in the attempt to determine the distribution of dialects in Common Indo-European — which is the object of the present book.

chapter eleven

The Voiceless Aspirated Stops

THE QUESTION OF THE VOICELESS ASPIRATED stops is a difficult one, since the type is relatively uncommon in Indo-European and examples showing their various developments are rather hard to find. However, the following facts seem certain:

(1) In Indo-Iranian, there is a series of sounds that are clearly distinct from the voiceless stops and that are realized in Sanskrit as voiceless aspirated stops and in Iranian as spirants: Skr. *kh* = Iran. *x*, Skr. *th* = Iran. *θ*, Skr. *ph* = Iran. *f*.

After *s* and *n*, Iranian has only voiceless stops; thus, *st* = Skr. *sth*, *nt* = Skr. *nth*. There is no ancient prepalatal series parallel to Skr. *ç* = Av. *s*, Skr. *j* = Av. *z*, Skr. *h* = Av. *z*. Sanskrit *kh* does not undergo a shift to affricate articulation before prepalatal vowels or before *y*, as shown by the example *khyāti* 'he sees'. Nor does the alternation of Skr. *k* and *c*, *g* and *j*, *gh* and *h*, have any parallel for *kh*. Sanskrit *ch*, which is in principle a double consonant anyway,

never represents either IE. *k_1h of the series Skr. *ç, j, h,*
or a liquid *kh before a prepalatal vowel.

(2) The Armenian equivalents of these Indo-Iranian
sounds are *x, th, ph.* The developments *x* and *ph,* which are
not found for IE. *k and *p, are eminently characteristic of
the Indo-European voiceless aspirated stops. However, the
Armenian development of *th* from IE. *th merges with the
Armenian outcome of IE. *t. A difference appears only
after *r:* while IE. *rt gives Arm. *rd,* IE. *rth gives Arm. *rth.*
This difference is very important; if the original pure
voiceless stops give voiced stops in Armenian after *r* and
after a nasal, it is because the consonant shift transforming
the pure voiceless stops into voiceless aspirated stops trans-
formed them at the same time into soft consonants capable
of becoming voiced; the original voiced aspirated stops,
however, remained strong. This explains how IE. *p became *h,* while IE. *ph is represented by Arm. *ph.* If Gr. έρφος
and Arm. *erphn* are indeed cognates—as indicated by H.
Pedersen (*KZ,* XXXIX, 363)—then *ph* clearly survives after
r, as does the *th* resulting from IE. *th. Only the Indo-
European guttural *kh is represented by an Armenian
spirant, *x.* The point is that gutturals have the possibility
of becoming spirants in cases where the other stops remain
stops. Thus, *g* becomes a spirant in Czech and Ruthenian,
and *ǧ* in Arabic; the treatment of *g* is also quite special in
some of the Germanic dialects. This is, then, a development peculiar to gutturals, which has no particular bearing
on the question of the Indo-European voiceless aspirated
stops.

To judge by Armenian, the Indo-European voiceless
aspirated stops were apparently quite a different thing from
the soft voiceless aspirated stops that we may observe today
in the pronunciation of many modern Germanic and
Armenian dialects. This is congruent with the preservation of *kh* before *$\breve{i}$, *y, and *$\breve{e}$ in Sanskrit.

Armenian does not attest, any more than Indo-Iranian does, the existence of a voiceless aspirated stop in the Indo-European prepalatal series represented in Armenian by *s, c, j, h.*

(3) In the case of Greek, two equivalences are certain: χ = Skr. *kh,* Iran. *x,* Arm. *x* and φ = S kr. *ph,* Iran. *f,* Arm. *ph.*

There is no voiceless aspirated stop attested in the labiovelar series.

As for **th,* the same certainty does not exist. There is a series of examples supporting the correspondence τ = Skr. *th,* Iran. θ, Arm. *th* (even after *r*), but there are some others tending to indicate the development θ, which parallelism would lead us to expect. The principal facts will be examined below.

(4) Slavic combines IE. **th* and **t, *ph* and **p* in *t* and *p.* The hypothesis has been advanced that IE. **kh* gives Sl. *x,* but it has been rejected by C. Uhlenbeck (*IF*, XVII, 95 and 177), who believes that **kh* is represented by *k,* just as **ph* and **th* are represented by Sl. *p* and *t;* since a guttural is here at issue, however, a break in parallelism would not be surprising. Unfortunately, there is no example that is really decisive either way; there is no sure example of IE. **kh* giving Sl. *k,* and there are several satisfying etymologies that would lead us to believe probable the development of Sl. *x* from IE. **kh.*[1]

(5) In Baltic, Germanic, Celtic, and Italic, the pure and aspirated types of voiceless stops fall together completely. The Latin development has been clearly outlined by Uhlenbeck (*IF*, XIII, 213), though some doubt has been raised by Pedersen (*KZ*, LX, 178).

Indo-European voiceless aspirated stops, then, tend to merge with the pure type, and the fusion is total in a continuous series of dialects. We are thus reduced to a very small group of languages for the study of these sounds.

The examples relative to *ph* and *kh* are known and are clear enough not to warrant enumeration here. Let us note only the two which most strongly support the hypothesis of *x*–development in Slavic:

Skr. *çákhā* 'branch', Pers. *šāx*, Arm. *çax*, Lith. *szakà;* Lith. *szakà* and OSl. *soxa* are apparently cognates, though this has been disputed by all the scholars examining these words recently.[2]

Skr. *kákhati* 'he laughs heartily', Arm. *xaxankh*, Gr. καχάζω, OSl. *xoxotŭ;* this is an onomatopoeia, as is—in the case of *ph*—the series Skr. *phut-karoti* 'he breathes, blows', Arm. *phukh* 'breath, puff', Gr. φῦσα, Lith. *pūsti*, OSl. *pyxati*, Lat. *pustula,* but this does not interfere with the application of phonological laws.

The relation of OSl. *plěšĭ*, Russ. *plêxán*, etc., to Lith. *plìkas* can be explained only on the assumption that *kh* is represented in Slavic by *x*.[3]

Examples tending to illustrate the Greek outcome of IE. *th* need closer examination:

Skr. *pŗthukaḥ* 'young animal', Arm. *orth* 'calf' (*th* after *r*), Gr. πόρτις, πόρταξ. This example is very important, since it is the only one in which IE. *th* is attested with any certainty by the agreement of two languages; in all other cases, *th* is attested only by Indo-Iranian.

Greek πλατύς cannot be isolated from Skr. *pŗthúḥ* 'wide', Av. *pərəθuš*, nor can πλάτος (with the vocalism of πλατύς) be separated from Skr. *práthaḥ*, Av. *fraθo* 'width'; Arm. *yałth* 'large, enormous', *yałthem* 'I triumph (over)', with *th,* would be comparable phonologically, but the meaning causes difficulty. The proper noun Πλαταιαί is inseparable from Skr. *pŗthivī* 'earth' and from Gaul. *Litavia*, OWel. *Litau*, Wel. *Llydaw* 'Armorica'. πλαταμών recalls Skr. *prathimán*-. πλάτη 'flat end of an object' is isolated (cf., however, Lat. *planta* 'sole of the foot' and the Sanskrit masculine form *pŗtháḥ* 'flat of the hand', like Gr. πλατεῖα), but ὠμο-πλάτη recalls

OSl. *plešte* 'shoulder'. πλάτανος (name of a tree) is the same as Gaul. *litano-*, OWel. *litan*, OIr. *lethan*. For θ, there is πλάθανος 'pastry board', but this isolated word cannot be given greater value than the cognates above; the *dh* could be an extension, comparable to other extensions of *pol-*, for example OIce. *flatr*, OHG. *flaz* (with *d*); moreover, πλάθανος allows for a different etymology.[4]

πετάννῡμι, πέτασα and πέταλος, πέταλον, πατάνη; cf. Av. *paθana-* 'stretched out', Oss. *fätän* (intervocalic *t* is represented by *d* in Ossetic[5]), Pers. *pahm*. This family of words not being represented in Sanskrit, *th* is attested only in Iranian. Elsewhere there can only be *t:* Lat. *pateō*, Lith. *petỹs* 'shoulder', OE. *fæđm* 'extension of both arms' (i.e., 'fathom'), etc.

πάτος 'road' and πόντος 'sea' have been linked to Skr. *pánthāḥ, patháḥ, pathibhiḥ*, Av. *pantåo, paθō* 'road', OSl. *pǫti*, OPruss. *pintis*, Lat. *pons* (*pontis*), Arm. *hun* (with disappearance of the dental).

τετρατός; cf. Skr. *caturtháḥ* 'fourth'; but here the suffix might be *-to-* in Greek; likewise, there is no way to determine the extent to which the Greek suffix for abstract nouns such as θάνατος is related to the Sanskrit suffix -*tha-* (= Av. -θa-) or the Sanskrit suffix -*ta-* (= Av. -*ta-*).

στᾱ- (in ἵστημι, ἔστην, etc.); cf. Skr. *sthā-*. The *t* of the other languages is ambiguous: Av. *stā-*, Lat. *stā-*, Germ. *stō-*, Lith. *sto-*, OSl. *sta-*. One might wonder whether the Greek τ depends perhaps on the preceding σ, but σ does not have such influence. A σφ- corresponds to Skr. *sph-*, Arm. *sph-* in σφαραγέω (cf. Skr. *sphūrjati* and Lat. *spargō*) and in σφυρόν, σφῦρα (cf. Skr. *sphurati* and Arm. *sphrem*).

στέγω and τέγος; cf. Skr. *sthágati* and Lith. *stógas*, Lat. *tegō* and *toga*, OIce. *þak*.

ἥδιστος; cf. Skr. *svādiṣṭhaḥ* and OHG. *suozisto*.

In cases where Greek θ seems to correspond to Skr. *th*, Av. θ, we see one of those Indo-European alternations of voiced and voiceless aspirated stops for which Skr. *nakhám* and Pers. *nāxun,* in comparison with OSl. *nogŭtĭ,* OHG. *nagal,* Lat. *unguis,* etc., provide an indisputable example.

Thus we have Gr. ϝοῖσ-θα alongside Skr. *vét-tha,* Goth. *wais-t* and Av. *dadā-θa,* Lat. *(tutudis-)tī.* There is an alternation of *dh* and *th* here, like the alternation between the 2nd-person plural active Skr. *-tha-* = GAv. *-θā* and the 2nd-person plural middle voice primary Skr. *-dhve* = GAv. *-duyē,* secondary *-dhvam* = GAv. *-dūm.* We even find an example of 2nd-person plural middle Av. *-θwe,* but the θ may be merely an orthographical substitution for δ.

A less surprising example of the alternation of **dh* and **th* is provided by Gr. ἀ-σκηθής in comparison with Goth. *skaþis* 'damage, harm', Ir. *scathaim* 'I damage'. Be it noted that the *th* is not directly attested, since the voiceless term in the pair is encountered only in the Western group.

Finally, there are certain false etymologies to correct, such as Gr. μόθος 'tumult of battle' alongside Skr. *mathnáti, mánthati,* OSl. *mętą,* Lith. *mentùrė,* OIce. *mǫndull.* The root attested in Indo-Iranian, Slavic, and Baltic has the primary meaning 'stir (up) a liquid', but it does not, in those languages, extend its meaning to include 'tumult of battle'. Moreover, the Greek word has *-o-,* without a nasal; and a nasal is one of the constituents of the root. The hypothesis, proposed by Ehrlich (*KZ,* XLI, 288), of contamination of **μονθος* and **μαθος* is confused, for thematic nouns do not undergo presuffixal vowel-gradation in the course of flection. Of the other words cited by Ehrlich, only one would cause some difficulty for the thesis advanced here: μονθυλεύειν· τὸ μολύνοντα ταράττειν (Phrynichus). However, this isolated word, whose formation is unclear, has nothing decisive about it; moreover, the θ may be based on **dh* alternating with **th;* no example of Gr. θ is probative under these conditions. As for the form *manfar* in Italic,[6] the *f* is a sufficient indication that the word ought not to

be considered here, and *a*–vocalism is no less unaccept-
able.

Thus, Indo-European voiceless aspirated stops are completely attested only in Indo-Iranian and Armenian. In
Greek, **t* and **th* fall together. Slavic distinguishes at most
*k and **kh*. The Western dialects show complete fusion. We
see here a development common to the Western dialects,
including Baltic and even Slavic, but at least partly exclud-
ing Greek, which clearly preserves two of the three voiceless aspirated stops whose existence is established by the
concordance of Indo-Iranian and Armenian.

chapter twelve

The Sibilant *s

THERE ARE TWO PHENOMENA TO BE CONSID-
ered here: the shift from *s to š and the shift from *s to h.

(1) In Indo-Iranian, *s becomes š and *z becomes ž after
i, u, r (representing r and l), and k, whether the sibilant is
followed by a vowel or a consonant or is in final position.[1]

In Slavic, *s is represented by the voiceless guttural
spirant x (no doubt representing an older š) after IE. *i, *u,
*r, *k (or rather, East Indo-European, for *k_1s gives s), but
only before a following vowel. This means that there are no
examples of IE. *-z- becoming *ž, etc., since z is not found
in Indo-European except before a voiced consonant. The
detailed demonstration is presented in an article by H.
Pedersen (*IF*, V, 33), which has been challenged, however,
by C. Uhlenbeck, who had originally supported the same
argument as Pedersen. Uhlenbeck (*KZ*, XXXIX, 599)
observes that the Slavic and Indo-Iranian laws do not have
the same breadth; Slavic contrasts *praxŭ* and *prŭsti* 'dust':

Indo-Iranian would have š in both cases; *s becomes š after II. *i* representing IE. *ə, which is a development peculiar to Indo-Iranian, etc. But the fact is that this is a matter of phenomena realized independently, in the Indo-European stage, by dialects of which some were to become Indo-Iranian and others were to become Slavic; a like manner of development is not inevitable in such a case, just as it is not inevitable in any of the events considered here. Uhlenbeck observes occurrences of Sl. *x* after *e, o, a;* they may all, however, be analogical: the final *i* of OSl. *bereši* is sufficient to rule out complete identification with Skr. *bhárasi* 'you bear'.² Finally, there are cases in which Uhlenbeck would have IE. *rs give Sl. *rz;* however, this development would be irreconcilable with certain proven examples where *rs gives Sl. *rx,* and the cases of *rz* must be explained as contaminations, as in *drŭzŭ* 'bold', compared with Gr. $\theta\rho\alpha\sigma\acute{v}\varsigma$, Skr. *dhr̥snúh.* In no case is it possible to accept *rs giving Sl. *rz,* for the original voiceless consonants are preserved in Slavic with absolute fixity and no such voicing is known in Common Slavic.

Even if we consider a Slavic shift from *s* to *z* acceptable under certain conditions, there would still be no grounds for denying the relation between II. š and Sl. *x,* as shown by Pedersen (*KZ*, XL, 179). If it is a matter of an Indo-European dialectal phenomenon, then the Indo-Iranian and Slavic innovations must be parallel.³

Lithuanian, too, has š after *i, u, r, k,* but it also shows *s* in the same environment, and there has not been any successful rigorous determination of the distributional pattern of *s* and š; it is not known, for example, why Lith. *blusà* = OSl. *blŭxa,* but Lith. *vētuszas* = OSl. *vetŭxŭ.*

The Old Prussian Encheiridion has a few isolated examples of *-rsch-* beside *-rs-,* notably *pirschdau* alongside *pirsdau,* and *pogirschnan* alongside *pogirsnan.*⁴ We might also cite *uschts* 'sixth'; cf. Skr. *ṣaṣṭháḥ;* the zero-grade of the presuffixal element in the Old Prussian word is correct from the Indo-European point of view.

For Armenian, it is difficult to find any valid evidence. The examples *tharšam* and *garšim* have been rejected by Pedersen (*KZ*, XXXIX, 413), and, indeed, **rs* gives Arm. *ṙ* in sure cases such as *oṙ* = OHG. *ars,* Gr. ὄρρος and *thaṙam* 'dry', synonymous with *tharšam*. It seems, however, that *c̣,* representing IE: **ks,* passed through a palatal fricative stage; otherwise there would be no adequate explanation of Arm. *veš-tasan* 'sixteen' in comparison with *vec̣* 'six' (cf. Gr. ʹϝέξ). When the *š* of *veštasan* became fixed, the pronunciation must have been something like **č̣.* (The *č̣* which is historically attested in a series of words results, on the other hand, from later changes.) Likewise, *arǰ* 'bear', the cognate of Skr. *ŕ̥kṣaḥ,* Gr. ἄρκτος, etc., changed to voiced *ǰ* the old **č̣* corresponding to Skr. *kṣ* and Gr. κτ before the *č̣* lost its palatal fricative articulation, whence *arǰ* alongside *vec̣* 'six'. It is not known whether *ǰ* here is related to **-ksy-,* since there is no trace anywhere of a **y* in the noun for 'bear' (Lat. *ursus,* Ir. *art,* etc.), and nothing proves that **-ksy-* gave *ǰ,* for the connection of Arm. *aj* 'right' with Gr. ἄξιος is not as certain as the connection with Skr. *sādhúḥ* more recently proposed by E. Lidén, *Armenische Studien* (Göteborg, 1906), p. 75. There is thus some trace of *š* in Armenian, at least after a guttural.

The change from **s* to *š* under certain conditions is, then, regular in Indo-Iranian. In Slavic it is severely limited (because, perhaps, of a return from *š* to *s* when *š* became *x*). In Baltic it is only partial. In Armenian there are, for the most part, only doubtful or disputed traces. As for Albanian, it is difficult to affirm anything because the treatment of **s* is very complicated in that language. And as for the other languages, they show no *s* represented by an early palatal fricative that might be of Indo-European

date. The *s*/*š* isogloss coincides in general with that of the
gutturals; this is important, for in both cases the Eastern
dialects show parallel innovation.

(2) The shift from *s to *h,* which is a simple phenomenon
of consonant opening, took place quite independently in
Celtic. Initial *s*- is generally retained in Gaulish and Irish;
nevertheless, in unstressed words, *s* became *h* in Irish and
then fell, whence the contrast between OIr. *samail* 'resemblance' and *amail* (*amal*) 'like'. In the Brythonic dialects,
the change from initial *s* to *h* is regular before a vowel.

In three Indo-European languages, whose grouping is
significant — Greek, Armenian, and Iranian — the shift from
s to *h* occurred not, as in Brythonic, at a relatively recent
date, but before the date of the oldest texts. Moreover, in
all three the distributional pattern is exactly the same: *h*
develops from initial *s before a vowel, from intervocalic
*s and from some occurrences of *s before and after
sonants; *s remains before and after a stop.

In the case of Iranian, the shift from *s to *h* antedates
the Achaemenian inscriptions, the Gathas, and the earliest
Greek transcriptions of Iranian names, e.g., Ἰνδός. [5]

In Armenian the change from *s to *h* is not merely
earlier than the most ancient texts; indeed, at the time of
those texts, *h* from *s had already fallen without exception
in intervocalic position and had fallen in most cases in
initial position, as in *ewthn* 'seven', *omn* 'someone' (cf. Goth.
sama 'same', *sums* 'someone'), *am* 'year'. Where *h* is retained,
as in *hin* 'old', we may wonder whether it is etymologically
more correct than the *h* of *hum* 'raw' (cf. Gr. ὠμός, Skr.
āmáḥ, Ir. *om*), *han* 'grandmother' (cf. Lat. *anus,* OHG. -*anna,*
Gr. ἀννίς), *haw* 'grandfather' (cf. Lat. *avus,* OPruss. *awis*),
haw 'bird' (cf. Lat. *avis*), *hasanel* 'arrive' (cf. Skr. *açnóti*), etc.
The *h* coming from initial *p, on the other hand, is almost
always preserved, as in *heru, het* (but *otn*), *hur, hayr,* etc.

In Greek the shift from **s* to *h* also antedates considerably the historical period. There is no trace of intervocalic *h* in any dialect; initial *h* (rough breathing) is retained in some dialects, but in many others it disappeared even before the period of the first epigraphic and literary texts.[6]

The occurrence of this shift from **s* to *h* in three neighboring languages and under like conditions would indicate dialectal origin of Indo-European date. It is, however, a relatively recent Indo-European phenomenon, as is indicated by the following two facts:

First, the change from intervocalic **s* to *h* in Iranian postdates the change from **s* to *š* after *i* and *u:* Iranian has *iša, uša,* and not *iha, uha.* Thus, if the shift is of Indo-European date, it occurred autonomously in each dialect, like all the other changes considered. This point should never be forgotten.

Secondly, the assimilation of initial **s* to an original prepalatal antedates the shift from initial **s* to *h* before *w* in Armenian, as is shown by Arm. *skesur* 'mother-in-law'; cf. Gr. ʿ*ϝεκυρά͂,* Av. *xvasura-.* (Lith. *szēszuras* and Skr. *çváçuraḥ* underwent the same assimilation as Armenian.) That this assimilation did not occur in Iranian is indicated by Av. *xvasura-.*

(Add.) The shift from **s* to *h* in initial and intervocalic position, as observed in Iranian, Armenian, and Greek, does not constitute any proof of a special relation among the Indo-European ancestors of these three languages. The shift is no more than one of the signs of the weakness of consonant articulation that characterizes all three.[7]

There is no reason, either, to ascribe any particular significance to the contrast between the relatively strong articulation of sibilants before a stop in Iranian, Armenian, Slavic, and Greek, and the relatively weak articulation of the same consonants in Indic on the one hand and in Italic and especially Celtic on the other.[8] The divergence in this respect of dialects as closely linked as Indic and Iranian seems to rule out a dialect division going back to Indo-European time.

chapter thirteen

The Germanic and Armenian Consonant Shifts

GERMANIC AND ARMENIAN SHOW CONSONANT shifts that are in every way alike. The symmetry of the two languages, originally pointed out by this writer (*MSL*, VII, 161 and *Esquisse d'une grammaire comparée de l'arménien classique* [Vienna, 1903], p. 7ff.), was questioned by Hübschmann (*Arm. Gram.*, p. 407ff.), but it has since been completely confirmed in the detailed study by H. Pedersen (*KZ*, XXXIX, 334) and by new evidence presented by Lidén (*Arm. Stud.*). It will here be considered firmly established.

Almost nothing can be said about the Indo-European voiced aspirated stops. In the case of Germanic, the statement is usually made that IE. **gh*, **dh*, and **bh* are represented by the voiced spirants γ, *đ*, and *ƀ*, but the proofs upon which that statement is based are hardly decisive. It is supported by the apparently certain fact that Common

Germanic had γ, đ, ƀ in intervocalic position; there is a general tendency, however, for intervocalic consonants to open, and spirant pronunciation of intervocalic voiced stops is found in Iranian, Armenian, and Irish as well. Moreover, the opening of intervocalic consonants is one of the more curious features of the developmental parallelism (autonomous) of each of the Western dialects (other than Greek); the spirant pronunciation of the Germanic voiced stops is only a special case of such opening. Opening of intervocalic stops shows up in various places and ways in Latin (and then, in different degrees, in each of the Romance languages), Oscan and Umbrian, the Celtic dialects (differently in Brythonic and Gaelic) and the Germanic dialects (especially in the form of voicing of intervocalic stops). On the other hand, Greek and particularly Baltic and Slavic generally treat intervocalic and initial stops in the same way; indeed, the preservation of intervocalic consonants is one of the most original features of the three languages. As for the question of initial stops, no inference is to be drawn from the intervocalic development of spirants representing in Germanic the voiced aspirated stops of Indo-European.

The usual statement about the Germanic outcome of IE. *gh, *dh, *bh is further supported by the observation that certain West Germanic dialects, notably Old English, have a spirant *g* even in initial position. But *g* is generally subject to spirant development in cases where the other voiced stops do not change, as in Czech, Ruthenian, or Arabic. There is therefore no reason to believe that *bh, *dh, and *gh are represented by spirants in Common Germanic; where spirants are found, known facts of general phonetics permit us to explain them easily as stemming from Common Germanic *b, d,* and *g.*

The Armenian consonants transcribed as *b, d, g, ǰ,* and *j* are voiced; they no doubt had certain features of glottal

emission which are not easy to define.[1] Intervocalic *b* became the spirant which is written as *v* or *w* according to the
preceding vowel.

Leaving aside the voiced aspirated stops, which are of
no special interest, and the voiceless aspirated stops, which
have already been discussed, we see that Armenian and
Germanic together exhibit two innovations:

(1) The voiced stops *b, *d, *g are represented by voiceless stops: Goth. *p, t, k, q;* Arm. *p, t, c, k.* The Armenian
voiceless stops must have been soft, rather than strong,
consonants, to judge by the modern dialects, some of which
have soft voiceless stops (Eastern type) whereas the others
have voiced stops (Western type).

(2) The original voiceless stops are represented in
Armenian by soft voiceless aspirated stops: *th* and *kh*. Soft
ph gives initial *h* and intervocalic *w, v;* the prepalatal $*k_1$
gives *s*. Common Germanic no longer had the soft voiceless
aspirated stops that Armenian still had in part; they had
given way to the voiceless spirants *x* (whence Goth. *h*), þ,
and *f*. The difference is the same as between Gr. φ, θ, χ,
and Lat. *f, h* (which correspond to Skr. *bh, dh, gh, h*). In
intervocalic position, the spirants are voiced; voicing is
prevented after a tonic vowel in the initial syllable (Verner's
law, which is proved only for this very special case of the
beginning of a word); after other vowels, the conditions of
voicing have not been defined in most dialects. In Gothic,
voicing does not occur when a voiced consonant begins the
preceding syllable (the Wrede–Thurneysen law).

The principle underlying the Armenian phenomenon
and the Germanic one is the same, even if we find attested
in Germanic only a relatively advanced phase of the development of which Armenian still shows almost the beginning. The essential change of the voiced and voiceless
consonants may be stated in a single formula: the glottal

vibrations are delayed with respect to the explosion of the stop.[2] Thereupon, the voiceless stops, which — according to the evidence of all Indo-European languages other than Germanic and Armenian — were strong and not aspirated, become aspirated. The glottal vibrations, instead of beginning immediately after explosion, without any interval (as occurs today, for example, in most Romance and Slavic languages), do not begin until later, and a voiceless breath sound is inserted between the explosion and the beginning of the vowel. Thus, *t* becomes *th* and *k* becomes *kh* (ancient Armenian). These aspirated sounds are soft, articulated without intensity, almost like voiced stops. Then they may voice under certain conditions (after *n* and *r* in Armenian, or in unstressed words such as the Armenian demonstrative *da* '[Lat.] iste' or the Armenian pronoun *du* 'you'[3]) or they may become spirants (Germanic). As for the Indo-European voiced stops, the glottal vibrations no doubt began at the very moment of implosion, as is still true today in most Romance and Slavic languages. Delayed in Germanic and Armenian, they would begin at the moment of explosion. The voiced stops thus reached the stage of soft voiceless stops, which is the stage represented by Armenian; further development made them strong in Germanic.[4]

The concordance of the Armenian and Germanic shifts is total, and it is very tempting to see the point of departure as a dialectal innovation of the Indo-European period. The first objections to arise may be met as follows:

(1) Armenian and Germanic were spoken in widely separated regions at the time of their appearance in history. However, Armenian had surely been carried far from its place of origin and had taken the place of a quite different earlier language, attested by cuneiform inscriptions (the Vanic inscriptions). Moreover, according to

historical findings, neither confirmed nor denied by linguistic evidence, the Armenians were descended from the
Phrygians, and the Phrygians from the Thracians.⁵ (Nevertheless, the vestiges of Phrygian and Thracian that we have
offer no indication of a consonant shift even in its initial
stage.)

(2) Certain words borrowed from neighboring languages underwent the consonant shift; thus, the Gaulish
proper noun *Volcae* is represented by OHG. *Walah,* OE.
Wealh; the Achaemenian word **paridaiza-* 'garden' (Av.
pairidaēza-, Gr. παράδεισος) provided Arm. *partēz* (with a *t*
and not a *d*). However, it is easy to see that, at a given
moment, **kh* should have been the prehistoric Germanic
sound most closely rendering a Gaulish *k;* from **kh* came
Germanic *x,* and then *h.* It is likewise easy to see that the
soft voiceless stop *t* should have been the Armenian sound
most closely rendering the Iranian voiced stop *d* in certain
cases. These borrowings, then, do not prove that the Germanic and Armenian consonant shifts could not have been
of Indo-European origin. In addition, the Runic alphabet,
as ancient as it is, already gives evidence of the completion
of the first stage of the shift.⁶

Those objections met, it is nevertheless true that there
is no decisive reason to see the two shifts as stemming from
an Indo-European dialectal event. First, only two languages are involved; the concordance is therefore minimally probative. Then, consonant shifts are not rare
occurrences or at all peculiar to the two languages in question: the Bantu dialects show quite similar shifts; the unstressed voiceless stops of Semitic appear in Aramaic as
aspirates (spirants in intervocalic position). But above all,
the consonant shifts in Germanic and Armenian, unlike
all the phonological developments studied in the preceding chapters, do not appear as the vestiges of very early
phonetic changes that have ended though their effects

survive. The tendencies expressed in the Germanic and Armenian consonant shifts arose before the historical period, but they then continued to be operative and have indeed persisted in part to the present day. High German has undergone a second shift. And the aspirate (or affricate) pronunciation of the voiceless stops *p, t, k* — together with the partial unvoicing of the stops *b, d, g* — in English and Danish really constitutes, too, a second shift, which, though less obvious than that of High German, is no less real. In German itself, the aspiration of the voiceless stops and the unvoicing of the other stops[7] constitute a third consonant shift. Certain Armenian dialects also show a second shift.[8] The persistence of such a tendency right up to the present day hardly indicates a very ancient date for the origin of the phenomenon.

It may easily be, then, that the shift took place independently in Armenian and Germanic. H. Hirt (*Indogermanen,* p. 616) has seen consonant shift as an immediate consequence of the development of stress accent. There are languages, however, that have very marked stress, e.g., Irish and modern Russian, and yet show no such shift; and the change from *p, t, k,* to *ph, th, kh* is only one element of consonant shift. The Tuscan developments described by F.-M. Josselyn, in his work on Italian phonology (*Parole,* IX, 602 and 833), show how such a phenomenon can occur. Josselyn observed in Siena an aspirate pronunciation of voiceless stops (which explains the development of spirants from the intervocalic voiceless stops in Tuscan) and an unvoicing of voiced stops (as in Germanic). Now Tuscan is Latin spoken by descendants of people whose language was Etruscan, and it is known that Etruscan did not have voiced stops. H. Schuchardt (*Slavodeutsches und Slavo-italienisches* [1885], p. 12ff.) has already indicated the hypothesis that certain peculiarities in Tuscan pronunciation of consonants are due to the survival of Etruscan articulatory habits. The consonant shift, then, could begin at the time when the Indo-European dialects that were to become Armenian and Germanic were adopted by foreign speakers accustomed to the aspiration of voiceless stops and unaccustomed to true voiced stops. The tendency has survived since then, producing new effects even today. If, as Hirt believes, the Germanic peoples occupy in part the area that was at one time the area of Common Indo-European, it does not necessarily follow that they have occupied that region uninterruptedly, or that they have not undergone some foreign invasion while yet preserving their language, or that they have not conquered and absorbed neighboring peoples. The facts are unknown, but there is no lack of possibilities that would give firm support to our hypothesis of substratum influence.

In the case of Armenian, Pedersen (*KZ,* XXXIX, 438) has rejected the hypothesis of Caucasian substratum influence. A question of such importance cannot be discussed in this limited space. It remains striking, however, that the Armenian system of stops and affricates, with its triple series of voiceless, voiceless aspirated, and voiced sounds, is the same as that of Georgian. And while certain languages show a change from p to f, or from g to γ, these alterations, peculiar to one or another isolated sound that was particularly exposed to change, are fundamentally different from the total shift characterizing Armenian no less than Germanic. Since Armenian provides the surest example of an Indo-European dialect occupying in historical time an area in which other languages were spoken earlier, the fact that it shows a consonant shift is significant and certainly seems to indicate the influence of a foreign substratum.

In his *Principes de linguistique psychologique* (Paris, 1905), p. 465ff., Father J. van Ginneken has presented in detail an analogous hypothesis for Germanic. He has made the

error, however, of attributing the origin of the consonant
shift to Celtic influence. There is no need here to determine whether Celtic could have had such a profound influence on Germanic: a few lexical borrowings (partly
questionable at that) never prove a strong linguistic influence. It suffices to observe that Celtic itself shows no trace
of a shift. Celtic shows an opening of intervocalic consonants, as Pedersen has pointed out; but this opening,
which occurred separately in each of the Celtic dialects,
has nothing in common with consonant shift, the principle
of which lies entirely in a retardation of glottal vibrations
with respect to stop explosion — which initial change leads
directly or indirectly to other phenomena. Thence result
a few resemblances, partial and wholly accidental, to certain phenomena in Irish, but all these ultimate complica-
tions must not be allowed to eclipse the initial event.
M. Bréal (*Revue de Paris,* XIV, No. 6, 59) has also attributed
the Germanic consonant shift to foreign influence, but has
not succeeded in specifying the influence — and it remains
enigmatic.

It is surely correct, then, to view the Germanic and
Armenian shifts as separate developments. The phonetic
possibilities involved are very limited in number, and the
realization of an identical possibility in two Indo-European
languages is not enough to permit the hypothesis of dialectal connection within Indo-European.

Armenian and Germanic belong, moreover, to two quite
different groups and present no other feature both held
in common and found nowhere else. There are some
striking morphological similarities, but these stem from
independent developments. Germanic and Armenian both
form the past participle and the infinitive by means of the
same suffix, but the suffix is *-no-* in Germanic (Goth.
baurans and *bairan*) and *-lo-* in Armenian (*bereal* and *berel*).
The infinitive is unique and derived from the present

stem; this is readily explained in Germanic: only the present stem has preserved its active participle, whereas the preterite stem does not have one. The same explanation must apply to Armenian, though in historical time the present active participle is no better attested than the preterite active participle. Such instances of parallelism in development do not establish dialect kinship.

chapter fourteen

The Augment

THE AUGMENT IS ATTESTED ONLY IN INDO-
Iranian, Armenian, and Greek; it is found nowhere else.

The absence of the augment from most of the area of
Indo-European can hardly be surprising, for even in the
languages in which it occurs, the earliest texts show only
an optional use of it. While it is normal in the Achaemenian
inscriptions, it is exceptional in the Avesta; in the ancient
Vedic texts it is often missing. Throughout the period in
which forms with the augment survive in Pali and the
Prakrits, the augment retains its optional character. In
ancient Greek the augment is necessary in all dialects; only
the Homeric language still has the possibility of not using
it—literary archaism thus preserving, in this case as in
others, linguistic habits that have disappeared from the
spoken language. In Vedic and in the Prakrits, as in the
language of Homer, it is mainly the length of the word
that tends to determine the presence or absence of the
augment.[1] What is only a tendency in these old texts, is
an absolute rule in ancient Armenian: the augment is
affixed to all consonant–initial verb forms which, if not

for this addition, would be monosyllables, e.g., *eber* 'he bore'= Gr. ἔφερε, Skr. *ábharat,* in contrast to *beri* 'I bore'; *etu* 'I gave', in contrast to *tuakh* 'we gave'. Since the monosyllabism of such a form as Arm. **ber* or *ac* 'he led' is due to the peculiarly Armenian fall of the final vowel, this rule indirectly attests the optional character of the augment in prehistoric Armenian, i.e., a state of the language comparable with that actually presented by Vedic and Homeric Greek.

The augment is not an essential element of the verb form. The proof, long known, is based on the Hellenic principle that, just as the accent cannot regress beyond the preverb immediately preceding the verb, so it cannot regress beyond the augment, whence παρ-έ-σχον no less than συμ-πρό-ες. The augment, then, is treated as a preverb, i.e., as a word that in Indo-European was wholly autonomous. Indeed, if the augment were really a part of the verb form, it would be a prefix; since there is no other prefix in Indo-European, the augment would thus constitute the only example of prefixing in the entire grammatical system of Indo-European.

The augment has survived for a very long time in each of the three languages in which it appears. Modern Greek still uses it regularly, despite the frequent fall of initial vowels that is so characteristic of this language. As much on its way toward disappearance as it may have been at the relatively late date of its attestation, Armenian did make regular use of the augment under the conditions already indicated, and if, by the Middle Ages, the language no longer possessed it, it is because Armenian gradually eliminated the forms in which the augment appeared, and achieved polysyllabism in all persons of the aorist in new ways. In India, the augment has always endured as long as the imperfect and aorist forms normally taking it; Pali and the Prakrits still have it. As for Iranian, the loss of the augment—naturally brought about by the substitution of participial forms for the personal forms—goes as far back as Pahlavi; yet in Yaghnobi, a remote dialect in which, exceptionally, the aorist has survived, the augment has also survived to the present day.[2] Despite its formerly optional and subsidiary character, the augment is, then, a stable element in the three groups of Indo-European languages possessing it.

It is therefore very significant that the augment is not found in any of the other Indo-European languages.

Since the augment is never a basic and necessary element of the verb form (or, at least, was not necessary until it became so in the course of the development of Sanskrit, Old Persian, Greek, and Armenian), there is no cause for surprise at its complete absence from a vast continuous area.

This absence is not due to any relatively recent fall. On the one hand, even under conditions leading us, on the basis of Indo-Iranian, Greek, and Armenian, to expect some trace of the augment, there is nothing of the kind in the languages in question, even in isolated form. On the other hand, the absence of the augment determined, or helped to determine, the development of verb forms.

The total absence of the augment in even the earliest texts, and in all the dialects of Italic, Celtic, Germanic, Baltic, and Slavic, is characteristic. Italic is known at a slightly less ancient stage than Indo-Iranian and Greek, but still before the Christian Era; and several quite distinct dialects of it are known. Yet even in the Duenos inscription we find a Latin preterite without the augment (*feced*), and not a single vestige of the augment is to be seen in Latin, Oscan, or Umbrian. The other languages are known at a later date but some, such as Gothic, Runic Norse, and Irish, are known at approximately the same date as Armenian; others, such as Old Prussian, Lithuanian, and the

Slavic dialects, appear with very archaic forms; in every
case we know a rather large number of dialects. And yet
nowhere is there any trace of the augment. At one time
it was thought that the augment could be discerned in
Goth. *iddja* 'I went', but no one believes that any longer.[3]
It is sufficient to contrast the universal lack of augment
from the earliest times and in all the dialects of these languages with the long survival of the augment in Greek,
Indo-Iranian, and Armenian to conclude that this morphological element was initially unknown throughout the
area here considered.

This is confirmed by an examination of the preterite
forms of the same languages. The secondary endings are
not sufficient to provide a clear contrast between the imperfect and the present; forms such as Hom. φέρομεν,
φέρετε are even wholly ambiguous in this respect. The imperfect and present system (Skr. *ábharam* alongside *bhárāmi*,
Gr. ἔφερον alongside φέρω) could not be maintained, then,
except in Indo-Iranian and Greek, i.e., in those languages
possessing the augment, capable of characterizing relatively unclear forms. Slavic still has traces of the imperfect,
but the forms serve an aorist function and they are only
isolated vestiges, viz., the few root aorists such as *padŭ*
'I fell', in comparison with *pade,* and the 2nd- and 3rd-
person forms of the type *nese,* which fill a lacuna in the
aorists in *-s-,* such as *něsŭ.* Slavic and Latin substituted new
forms, e.g., OSl. *neseaxŭ,* Lat. *ferēbam,* for the original imperfect which, without the augment, was not adequately
marked. In Irish the secondary endings were put to a quite
special use, serving to distinguish between conjunct inflection and absolute inflection.[4] A new form was created,
often called the secondary present, which is not a continuation of the original imperfect. Lithuanian created an
imperfect of habitual action, the type *sùkdavau,* as new as
Lat. *ferēbam* and OSl. *neseaxŭ.* Germanic does not have any-

thing taking the place of the imperfect. These same languages developed a preterite deriving from the Indo-European aorist and perfect, and presenting clear and well-defined characteristics, most of which are peculiar to each language. Forms such as Lat. *probāvī*, Osc. p r ú f a t t e d, OIr. *ro carus* 'I loved', Goth. *salboda* 'I rubbed with oil', Lith. *pāsakojau* 'I recounted', and OSl. *dělaxŭ* 'I did, made', all represent original formations in which the preterite is expressed independently of the secondary endings, and in which (as in Irish and Lithuanian) the distinction between primary and secondary endings may no longer play any role at all. Thus, the manner in which Italic, Celtic, Germanic, Baltic, and Slavic eliminated the imperfect and came to express the preterite presupposes an original, Indo-European, absence of the augment throughout this group of languages.

We thus have grounds for positing two distinct Indo-European dialect groups, and this shows that isoglosses may be drawn within Indo-European no less for morphological phenomena than for phonological. This is confirmed by the examination of a certain number of cases in which dialect distribution is a little less obvious.

chapter fifteen

The Perfect

THE INDO-EUROPEAN PERFECT IS IN EVERY respect a unique formation. It has a set of endings in the active and perhaps even in the middle voice that are peculiar to it, and an active–participle suffix (especially in the singular) that is likewise unique. The vowel preceding the ending of the active singular is -*o*- (and not -*e*-), unlike what we observe in most of the other athematic forms. (Nevertheless, OE. and OSax. *dōm*, OHG. *tuom* 'I do', and Arm. *utem* 'I eat' show that *o* was not entirely impossible in the athematic root present.) Reduplication regularly occurs with *e*, as in Gr. λέλοιπα, or else repeats an *i* or *u* found in the root, as in Skr. *tutude* = Lat. *tutudī*, Skr. *riréca*. Finally, the accent, instead of moving between the initial syllable of the stem and the ending, as in the present (Ved. *bíbharmi, bibhṛmási;* Gr. διδοῦναι, διδούς, but δίδοσθαι), moves between the syllable preceding the ending and the ending itself (Skr. *jajā́na, jajñúḥ;* Gr. λελεῖφθαι, λελειμμένος, like λελοιπέναι, λελοιπώς). The perfect is preserved as an autonomous formation only in Greek and Indo-Iranian, i.e., only in the oldest known and most archaic languages. This circumstance complicates the study of the dialect situation; yet, if we examine the Indo-European languages as a whole, similarities come to light that seem to indicate dialect distinctions with regard to the perfect.

In Greek and Indo-Iranian the perfect was first maintained in its original state, without any fundamental change. In Greek it was even extended: all verbs, including the denominatives, were given a perfect of the type τετίμηκα, a purely Greek creation. Then the form was eliminated; the modern Indic, Iranian, and Hellenic dialects have kept none of it, or almost none. Armenian is known at too late a stage for us to find the perfect preserved in it, but it does concord with the late Indo-Iranian and Hellenic dialects in showing the elimination to have been total — the perfect not having survived even in isolated cases or vestigially in other forms.

As for the other languages, from the very beginning of written tradition the perfect was no longer in existence as an autonomous form; however, its remains contributed in varying degrees to the formation of the preterite.

The languages in which the perfect combined with the aorist in the formation of a preterite are the same as those which never possessed the augment. The augment clearly distinguished the various forms of the preterite from the perfect and made any confusion impossible, for except in its own preterite (the quite rarely used pluperfect) the perfect made no use of the augment. Thus, the distinction between Indo-Iranian, Armenian, and Greek on the one hand, and all of the other languages on the other, is partly a consequence of the dialectal phenomenon examined in the preceding chapter.

There is surely another cause, however. In Greek and Indo-Iranian reduplication in the perfect is almost uni-

versal. In Greek it came to extend even to all derived
verbs; no longer having its original Indo-European character of partial reduplication of the root, it became simply
the repetition of the initial consonant of the verb, followed
by the vowel ε, as in πεφίληκα, τετίμηκα, δεδήλωκα, etc.
This transformation, which led at first to an extension
of the role of reduplication, led eventually to its disappearance by depriving it of its essential meaning: the
repetition of an initial consonant is meaningful only insofar as it is a shortened restatement of the root. The occurrences of Common Indo-European perfects without reduplication are isolated and few in number. The main
ones are found among roots beginning with w. The general
Indo-European example is Skr. véda, GAv. vaēdā, Gr.
ϝοῖδα, Goth. wait, OSl. vědě (and věmĭ), OPruss. waidimai,
Arm. gitem; Ionic has οἶκα in contrast to Hom.(ϝ)έ(ϝ)οικα;
Vedic has viçiván; Arm. gom 'I am' may be best explained
by taking as the point of departure a perfect corresponding
to Goth. was.[1] The grouping of these examples suggests
that the absence of reduplication may be related to the
special form of reduplication—without a vowel—that is
normal in Sanskrit roots with initial v, the type uváca, ūcúḥ.
The other examples cited[2] are not quite clear; they may
be explained in part by special circumstances, and all are
not perfects; their number is, in any case, negligible compared with that of Sanskrit forms with reduplication.

On the other hand, reduplication is often missing from
the vestiges of perfect forms that are to be found in
Slavic, Baltic, Germanic, Celtic, and Italic.

In Baltic and Slavic all that remains of the perfect is the
active participle, which is independent of the personal
forms of the preterite, the latter being based on the aorist.
This participle, which has the suffix of the perfect participle and a vocalism that is explained by the vocalism of the
Indo-European perfect, is always non-reduplicative, as in

Lith. *mìręs, mìrusi,* OSl. *-mĭrŭ, -mĭrŭši,* in contrast to Skr. *mamṛván, mamrúṣī.* The participles sometimes preserve a special root vocalism distinct from the stem vocalism of the infinitive, the aorist and even the present, e.g., OSl. *vlŭkŭ* and *brŭgŭ,* but they never show reduplication. The Baltic and Slavic forms are too isolated to prove the existence of non-reduplicative forms: a modern Greek participle such as βλαμμένος is based on βεβλαμμένος; nevertheless, forms such as *vlŭkŭ* and *brŭgŭ* in Old Slavic are archaic enough to give at least some indication.

The Germanic preterite is in large part derived from the Indo-European perfect, as is shown by the vocalism and final consonants of the singular, the type *man, warþ,* etc., in Gothic. But as a general rule, Gothic (almost the only Germanic dialect in which reduplicative forms ordinarily retained their clarity) has reduplication only where the preterite is not marked by some special *a*–vocalism (orig. *o*-): *stauta/*staistaut, halda/haihald,* etc. The only exceptions are a few verbs with *ē*–vocalism, such as *saia/saiso, teka/taitok,* but *slepa/saizlep* conforms to the general principle. It is hard to see why Germanic, in which the vocalism of the perfect is so well preserved, would have eliminated reduplication, unless it had ancient non-reduplicative models.

It might be said that the Germanic preterite results from a combination of perfects and root aorists: Goth. *budun* may be the 3rd-person plural of an athematic root aorist, and OHG. *liwi* is surely the 2nd-person singular of a thematic root aorist. However, there is a category that — given its meaning — excludes any possible mixture of aorists, and which, in fact, has the West Germanic perfect ending *-t* in the 2nd-person singular, rather than the aorist form of the type OHG. *liwi* (which was generalized in the preterite in a Germanic group). The category is that of the preterite–presents. These preterite–presents, which are

pure perfects in both form and meaning, never show reduplication; thus, Goth. *man,* OE. *man* (2nd pers. *manst*), in
contrast to Gr. μέμονα; Goth. þarf, OHG. *darf* (2nd pers.
darft), etc. This clearly indicates that Germanic is based on
a dialect from which, as early as the Indo-European period,
reduplication was absent or could be absent.

Latin uses reduplication of the perfect to the same
extent, and in the same way, as Gothic. Reduplication
occurs when the vocalism of the perfectum is the same as
that of the infectum, as in *caedō/cecīdī, tangō/tetigī, canō/cecinī,
tundō/tutudī, mordeō/momordī,* etc. Forms such as *meminī* have
ambiguous vocalism. When the perfectum is characterized
by its vocalism, however, there is no reduplication—thus,
linquō/līquī, vincō/vīcī, fugiō/fūgī, frangō/frēgī, emō/ēmī, etc.;
there is no way of determining whether these forms are
based on original perfects or original aorists. The correspondences between Latin and Germanic pointed out by
H. Hirt (*IF,* XVII, 279) result, then, from the application
of a general principle, and they prove nothing individually.
But convergence of principle is more important than this
or that convergence of detail would be, and Hirt (*Ablaut,*
p. 196) was quite right to draw attention to the importance
of non-reduplicative perfect forms in the Western dialects.

Irish shows reduplication in the same cases as Latin and
Gothic:[3] *canim/cechain, gonim/gegon, cladim/cechladatar* (3rd-
pers. pl.), *maidim/memaid, nascim/-nenasc, tongu/-tetag, tuilim/
tetol.* There are a few examples, however, with preservation
of the vocalism of the perfect: *rigim/reraig, dingim/-dedach,
grennim/gegrainn, sennim/sefainn;* cf., from this point of
view, the type Goth. *taitok.* Nevertheless, in those cases
where the vocalism is *ō* (which became *ā* in Irish), i.e.,
where it is highly characteristic, the vocalism must be that
of the 3rd-person singular (Ved. *jajāna*) in opposition to
the 1st-person (*jajána*), but there is no reduplication, as in
guidim/ro gáid, techim/ro tāich, scuchim/ro scāich. Germanic has

forms of this kind only to the extent that the present has
a–vocalism (from **o*), e.g., OHG. *faru, fuor,* Goth. *graba,
grof,* etc. However, it may have had a large number of them,
for it preserves reduplication in cases where the preterite
singular is characterized by vocalic quality but could never
have been characterized by quantity, as in Goth. *teka, taitok.*
We may suspect that Germanic originally contrasted 1st-
person *bar* and 3rd-person **bōr* (cf. the Vedic contrasts
between *jabhára* and *jabhára*), and then, by analogy with the
type *band, warþ,* generalized *bar;* this offers a means, however doubtful and hypothetical, of explaining the contrast
between *bar* and *taitok.* In any case, the absence of reduplication which is characteristic of Germanic is in part encountered in Irish as well.

It is likely that the long vowel of the types OIr. *gād* and
Goth. *grof* has nothing to do with the *ē* of the type Goth.
setum, Lat. *sēdī;* Goth. *qemum,* Lat. *vēnī;* OHG. *brāhhum,* Lat.
frēgī, and of Lithuanian preterites such as *ēmė, vėrė,* etc.
The interpretation of these forms given by Loewe (*KZ,* XL,
289) is obviously erroneous—as is his understanding of Skr.
sedimá, which it is surprising to find cited together with
forms based on IE. **ē.* Since the preterite–presents show
zero-vocalism in the perfect—as in Goth. *munun, skulun,*
in contrast to the *ē*–grade of ordinary preterites such as
Goth. *qemun, berun*—these forms with *ē* are very possibly
from original aorists. Nowhere, indeed, do they have the
value of true perfects, and everywhere they act as preterites; the contrast between Goth. *munun* 'they think' and
qemun 'they came' seems decisive. And in that case, Lat.
vēnī, lēgī, etc., must also be considered as proceeding from
original aorists, just like OIr. *ro mīdar.*

Loewe (*KZ,* XL, 284) tries to account for non-reduplicative perfects by claiming a loss of reduplication through
haplology. The explanation is arbitrary and quite unlikely,
since the Western languages have forms both with and

without reduplication. The explanation is above all useless, however, for we do not know, and have no means of discovering, whether reduplication was ever universal in the Indo-European perfect.

One thing alone is certain: unlike Greek and Indo-Iranian, Slavic, Baltic, Germanic, Celtic, and perhaps Italic normally (and not sporadically) show, in certain cases, non-reduplicative forms that represent Indo-European perfects. We may thus explain that the perfect was less stable in all of those languages than it was in Indo-Iranian and, particularly, in Greek. Forms without reduplication are clearly of Indo-European origin, and it would be purposeless to try to determine whether they ever had reduplication or, having had it at a pre-Indo-European stage, they then lost it through the fall of *e.

Convergence of the perfect and the root aorist (especially of the athematic type), already possible through the absence of the augment, was thus facilitated in these dialects by the absence of reduplication in the perfect — and did indeed take place. The Latin perfectum is a combination of perfect and aorist, the details of which are well known; it is enough simply to mention forms such as dīxistī, tutudistī. In West Germanic the 2nd-person singular of the preterite is borrowed from the root aorist, while the 1st and 3rd come from the perfect, e.g., OHG. lēh (1st and 3rd pers.), liwi (2nd pers.). In the Germanic dialects we have no means of determining whether the preterite plural represents a perfect without the augment or a root aorist: Goth. budun is wholly ambiguous and may be related either to the perfect stem of Ved. bubudhé (minus the reduplication) or to the aorist stem of Ved. budhānáḥ; only the forms of the type Goth. qemun can be recognized as aorists with any degree of probability. In Irish the preterite of some verbs is an original aorist; in general, each verb has only one preterite; whatever its origin, then, the preterite of any given verb has the same function and sense as that of any other verb. Germanic, Celtic, and Italic show the common innovation of a general preterite (or perfectum) built upon a combination of perfect and aorist forms; Baltic and Slavic have an aorist indicative and a perfect active participle.

chapter sixteen

The Present Suffix *-ye-

THE INDO-IRANIAN PRESENT SUFFIX -*ya*- HAS
multiple functions, but a single form. The suffix is always
-*ya*-, whether it occurs in denominatives, e.g., Skr. *namasyáti,*
in deverbatives, e.g., Skr. *dediçyáte* (alongside *dédiṣṭe*), in
verbs of state, e.g., Skr. *mányate,* or in passives, e.g., Skr.
chidyáte.

The corresponding suffix in Greek is always -*γε/ο*-, whatever its use may be: τελείω, μαρμαίρω, σχίζω, μαίνομαι,
etc. The form of the Greek suffix coincides exactly with
that of the Indo-Iranian suffix.

In place of this apparently single suffix, Baltic and
Slavic have two distinct types. One occurs in verbs of state
characterized in the present by Sl. -*i*- (circumflex intonation) and Lith. -*i*- (short) in all persons except the first, e.g.,
OSl. *mĭnitŭ,* Lith. *mìni* (1st-pers. pl. *mìnime*); cf. Skr. *mányate*
and Gr. μαίνεται. The other occurs in presents that are
generally derived, i.e., in denominatives, such as OSl.
dĕlajǫ, Lith. *pãsakoju;* in deverbatives, such as OSl. *dajǫ,*

Lith. *jùngiu;* or ancient derivatives which later assumed the character of primary presents, such as OSl. *ližą,* Lith. *lëžiù.* This second type has the Slavic suffix *-je-,* the Lithuanian suffix *-ja-* in all persons.[1]

The two distinct suffixes *-ĭ-* and *-ye/o-,* attested by Slavic and Baltic, are also found in Armenian. Verbs of state and the passives derived from them, as in Indo-Iranian, are marked by *-i-;* the preceding consonants do not seem to undergo the changes usually effected by the am seated' (aorist *n-stay*) seems to have the same *-i-* as OSl. *sěditŭ* 'he is seated'. In no case do passives such as *berim* 'I am borne' (compared with *berem* 'I bear') show any trace of action by *y.* There are grounds, then, for believing that the suffix was *-ĭ-,* as in Baltic and Slavic. The suffix in denominatives and deverbatives, on the other hand, was *-ye-,* with consonantal *y;* examples: *gočem* 'I shout', from **wokʷ-ye-,* cf. Skr. *vắk* with genitive *vacáḥ,* Av. *vāxš* with instrumental *vača,* Greek accusative $(_F)ό\pi α$ and dative $(_F)ο\pi ί,$ Lat. *vōx,* cf. for the meaning Old Prussian vocative *wackis* 'outcry, (G.) Geschrei'; *kočem* 'I call', from **gʷot-ye-,* cf. Goth. *qiþan; ačem* 'I grow', cf. Lith. *úga* 'push, grow';[2] *čanačem* 'I know', with *-če-* based on IE. *-ske-* extended by *-ye-,* giving *-sk-ye-,* cf. Gr. *γνώσκω,* Lat. *(g)nōscō,* etc.

Slavic, Baltic, and Armenian, then, form a group of dialects which, with their distinction between *-ĭ-* and *-ye-* (*-yo-*), contrast with Indo-Iranian and Greek, in which *-ye-* (*-yo-*) is the only form attested for both types.

In Germanic and Italic the *-ĭ-*–type of Slavic, Baltic, and Armenian is apparently barely represented.

What remains of it in Latin is found mainly in derived verbs with the secondary suffix *-ske-,* such as Lat. *(re)mini-scor, (com-)mini-scor,* in contrast to OSl. *mĭni-tŭ,* Lith. *mìni.* These forms show nothing characteristic, for Greek also has derivatives in *-i-σκω,* such as *εὑρίσκω* (alongside *εὕρηκα*); even Iranian has Av. *γri-sa-.* The form with *-ē-,* which often occurs alongside these presents, is ordinarily the

only one to survive; Latin thus has *sedēre, sedeō* alongside
OSl. *sĕditŭ, sĕdĕti; vidēre, videō* alongside OSl. *viditŭ, vidĕti,*
etc.

On the other hand, at least in those cases where the
suffix follows a consonant, the presents corresponding to
the Slavic, Baltic, and Armenian type in *-ye-/-yo-* show, in
Germanic and Italic, an alternation of *-yo-* (in the forms,
or in some of the forms, in which the vowel preceding the
ending of the thematic type is *-o-*) and *-ĭ-*, the quantity
of the *i* being in part determined by that of the preceding
syllable. The Latin and Gothic forms are in perfect correspondence, except in the 1st-person plural, where there is
no way of knowing whether the Latin form or the Germanic represents the original type:

(1)	Lat.	*sāgiō*	*sāgīs*	*sāgit*	*sāgīmus*	*sāgītis*	*sāgiunt*
	Goth.	*sokja*	*sokeis*	*sokeiþ*	*sokjam*	*sokeiþ*	*sokjand*
(2)	Lat.	*capiō*	*capis*	*capit*	*capimus*	*capitis*	*capiunt*
	Goth.	*hafja*	*hafjis*	*hafjiþ*	*hafjam*	*hafjiþ*	*hafjand*

As is indicated by OHG. *hevis, hevit,* OSax. *hefis, hefid,* etc.,
the *j* of Goth. *hafjis, hafjiþ* stems from an analogical innovation peculiar to Gothic.[3] Osco-Umbrian tends to generalize
-ĭ-, as in Umbr. h e r i s, *heri;* nevertheless, a few synco-
pated forms, such as Umbr. h e r t e r and Osc. *factud,*
clearly indicate the existence of an *-ĭ-*form in Osco-
Umbrian.[4] Thus, the type that always shows *-ye-* in Slavic,
Baltic, and Armenian shows *-ĭ-* in Italic and Germanic —
at least in all forms for which the general rule of thematic-
type vocalism would call for *e.* Nor are we concerned here
with verbs of state; Lat. *habēre* and Goth. *haban* correspond
to Lith. *tùri, turéti* 'have' in meaning, and Lat. *capiō,* Goth.
hafja likewise correspond to Lith. *tvèria, tvérti* 'take'.

To the very limited extent that Germanic has forms
corresponding to the forms with *-ĭ-* in Baltic, Slavic, and
Armenian, the type merges completely with the preceding
type, that of Goth. *hafja.* Two certain examples (not attested in Gothic, however) are: OHG. *sizzu, sitzis* and *liccu,
ligis;* OSax. *sittia, sitis* and *liggiu, ligis;* OE. *sitte, sitest* and

licge, ligest; OIce. *sitja* and *ligja;* cf. OSl. *sěždǫ, sědiši* and
ležǫ, ležiši. Only Gothic has the forms *sitan* and *ligan,* which
may also be ancient; cf. Gr. λέχεται. Moreover, Old High
German has the present forms *hebis* (*hebist*), *hebit, libit, segit*
from *habēn, lebēn, sagēn* (cf. the type Lith. *tùri/turéti*); and
the 1st-person singular in OSax. *hebbiu,* OE. *hæbbe,* the
common form of the plural being OSax. *hebbiad,* OE.
habbađ, hæbbađ. Notable remnants, then, of the present
with *-ye-/-ǐ- survive, though the form with *-ē- tends to be
generalized.

In general, Germanic eliminates the type corresponding
to the Slavic type in *-i-;* thus the Gothic preterite–present,
man, etc., takes the place of the present corresponding to Sl.
minǫtǔ, for the preterite–present is, indeed, sometimes substituted for a present type not preserved in Germanic; see,
for example, Goth. *ga-dars,* etc., in comparison with Skr.
dhr̥ṣṇóti, OSl. *drǔznǫ* (and traces of *drǔznov-*).

Given the obvious inseparability of the Italic and Germanic phenomena, an equivalent ought to appear in Celtic
as well. Unfortunately, the state of phonological and morphological deterioration in which we find the earliest Celtic
dialects whose grammatical forms we know makes determination of the equivalent impossible in most cases.
There are, nevertheless, a few decisive forms in Old Irish.
The conjunct 3rd-person singulars *-gaib* 'he takes', on the
one hand, and *-lēici* 'he lets, leaves', on the other, are in fact
based on the finals *-ĭt (after a short syllable) and *-īt (after
a long syllable); and *-gaib* rules out *-yet, which would
result in OIr. *-i.* The 2nd-person singular imperatives
gaib 'take' and *lēic* 'let, leave' provide no indication of the
quantity of final *-i* (*-ī and *-ĭ having the same outcome in
Irish), but they do rule out *-ye; they are forms, then,
of the same type as Lat. *cape* (from *capi) and *sāgī.*
These Irish forms belong to verbs corresponding to the
type Sl. *-je-,* Lith. *-ja-* (cf. Lith. *tvèria* 'he takes'). There are
in Irish presents corresponding to the type Sl. *-i-,* Lith.

-i-, but they are deponents and thus include no forms, such as *gaib*, that would be instructive. The main ones are *moiniur* 'I think' and *gainiur* 'I am born'; everything occurs as if both types were fused, as in Germanic. Latin has *fīō*, *fīs*, which belongs to this type and behaves exactly like *sāgiō*, *sāgīs*.

Germanic, Celtic, and Italic are thus in perfect concordance, and we are justified in positing three distinct groups:

(1) Greek and Indo-Iranian, with the single suffix *-ye/yo-* serving for presents both of verbs of state and of derived verbs;

(2) Slavic, Baltic, and Armenian, with the suffix *-ĭ-* in presents of verbs of state, and the suffix *-ye/yo-* in derived verbs;

(3) Germanic, Celtic, and Italic, with the suffix *-yo-/-ĭ-* in derived verbs. There is a tendency in the third group to eliminate the type that would correspond to the Slavic, Baltic, and Armenian type in *-ĭ-*, and, to the limited extent of its survival, it merges here, in its form, with the type of the derived presents (Sl. *-je-*).[5]

chapter seventeen

A Few Noun Suffixes

THERE ARE SOME NOUN FORMATIONS THAT
are limited to certain dialects; examples follow.

(1) Thematic nouns of the type Gr. γόνος = Skr. *jánaḥ,*
Gr. φόρος = Skr. *bháraḥ,* and corresponding derivatives
with *-ā-,* such as Gr. φορά́, Lett. *(at-)bara,* Arm. *(thaga-)*
wora(-w) 'by the king' (lit., 'by the wearer of the crown'),
are frequent in Indo-Iranian, Slavic, Baltic, and Greek.
They have much less importance in Germanic; in Celtic
and Italic, they are represented only by a few words.

(2) The suffix **-tero-, *-toro-, *-tro-* serves in all Indo-
European languages to mark the opposition of two quali-
ties, but in only two languages, Greek and Indo-Iranian,
is the use of the suffix extended to include the formation
of secondary adjectival comparatives, type Gr. ὡμότερος =
Skr. *āmátaraḥ.* From the general function of the suffix
comes the independent Irish use of it in comparisons of
equality, e.g., OIr. *luathither* 'as swift', from *luath.* This
development, by its very difference, points to the significance of the Greek and Indo-Iranian convergence.

Latin, Irish, Germanic, Lithuanian, and Slavic, on the other hand, borrow their secondary comparative from the original primary type (Skr. *-yas-*, etc.); Armenian, which has a completely new formation, is not instructive in this respect.

(3) The suffix *-lo-*, as in Gr. σῑγηλός, μῑμηλός, Lat. *crēdulus, bibulus,* Goth. *sakuls* 'quarrelsome', *slahals* 'rowdy, brawler',[1] provides only two languages with participles: Slavic, in which the type *neslŭ,* accompanied by various auxiliaries, serves to form all compound tenses, and Armenian, in which there are both participles such as *bereal* (gen. *bereloy*) 'borne, having borne' and infinitives such as *berel* (gen. *bereloy*) 'bear', and in which there is no other past-participle or infinitive formation. Nevertheless, Umbrian may also present such a use of the suffix in the type *entelust* '(Lat.) imposuerit'; and in the Celtic dialects there are infinitives with *-l-*, notably in Breton,[2] but the development of the infinitive is a dialectal phenomenon in Celtic.

(4) The suffix of primary comparatives is extended by the suffix *-en-* in Greek, Germanic, and Lithuanian, as in Gr. ἡδίων, ἡδίονος (the form without extension survives in the Attic accusative ἡδίω, etc.), Goth. *sutiza, sutizins* (this is not a weak-declension adjective; the nasal is constant), Lith. *saldēs-n-is.*

Primary comparatives, unlike all other adjectives,[3] have no special feminine form in Greek, Italic, or Celtic. Thus, Gr. ἡδίων (and ἡδίω, etc.), Lat. *suāvior,* OIr. *siniu* 'older' serve both as masculine and as feminine forms. In Irish, given the additional fact of the limitation of the comparative to the nominative case, the form is invariable. A feminine comparative was developed in several contiguous dialects — Germanic, Slavic, and Indo-Iranian; in Baltic, the secondary suffix of the type Lith. *saldēs-n-i-s* made the introduction of a feminine form inevitable.

(5) The suffix *-tūt-* of adjective-derived nouns is found

in Italic, Celtic, and Germanic; examples are Lat. *iuventūs,*
-tūtis, OIr. *ōitiu, ōited* 'youth' and *bethu, bethad* 'life', Goth.
*mikildu*þ*s* 'size'. The suffix is widespread in Latin and in
Irish, but it is rare in Gothic and is not found in the other
Germanic languages. Just as with the type φόρος, φορά,
Germanic is midway here between Italo-Celtic and the
other Indo-European languages.

(6) The type of collective nouns of number, such as Skr.
trayáḥ, OSl. *troji (troje),* Lith. *treji̇̀,* is clearly attested only
in Indo-Iranian, Slavic, and Baltic. Traces found in the
other languages are all doubtful;[4] on the other hand, the
*-no–type of Lat. *trīnī, ternī* is found only in Italic, Germanic, and Baltic.[5]

(7) In Indo-European, **-o*–stem nouns could have feminine gender, as shown by Lat. *fāgus,* Gr. φηγός, νυός, and
Arm. *nu* (gen. *nuoy*), etc. Thus animal names with *-o*-stems
designated both males and females, as in Gr. ἄρκτος, ἵππος,
etc. Special nouns for female animals all represent independent developments in the various dialects of Indo-
European; sometimes the results of these developments
coincide in several languages, as in Skr. *áçvā,* Lith. *aszvà,*
Lat. *equa,* but often they also diverge, as in Skr. *ṛkṣī̀,* Lat.
ursa.[6] The feminine of the word for 'god' in Sanskrit is
devī́, in Latin *dea* (cf. Oscan dative deívaí). A feminine
in **-ā*- did not normally stand in contrast in Indo-European
to a masculine–neuter in **-e/o*-, except in the case of
adjectives. However, in all languages other than Italic,
Greek, and Armenian (before the loss of grammatical
gender in Armenian), the fact that in adjectives **-o*- was
the mark of the masculine and neuter (and contrasted with
feminine **-ā*-) brought about the elimination of feminine
gender from **-o*–stem nouns. Either the stem with **-o*-
was kept, but with its gender changed to masculine, as in
Skr. *bhūrjaḥ,* Lith. *bérzas* 'birch'; or feminine gender was
kept, but the stem class changed to **-ā*-, as in OSl. *brĕza,*

OIce. *biǫrk*.[7] Indo-Iranian, Slavic, Baltic, Germanic, and Celtic are alike in eliminating feminine gender from stems with *-o-.

K. Brugmann (*IF,* XXI, 315) rejects the idea that *-o-stems could have feminine gender in Indo-European. He challenges the value of the form *snusó-* with an etymology of his own;[8] but, aside from the fact that the explanation of an Indo-European word is not open to verification, it remains true that Indo-European has a word *snusó-* 'daughter-in-law', which means that Indo-European did have a stem in *-o-, designating a woman. More important is the fact that Brugmann does not question the reasons which make it seem probable, a priori, that stems with *-e/o- could occur with feminine gender. All other types of substantive stems allow for feminine gender; on the other hand, stems in *-ā- are not limited to the feminine, but provide masculine substantives as well in Latin (*scrība*), Greek, Slavic (*sluga, vojevoda,* etc.), and Armenian (*thagawor,* instrumental *thagaworaw* 'king'). Thus, Latin and Greek are representative of Indo-European usage rather than departures from it. Moreover, it is hardly likely that the feminine gender of words such as Gr. ὁδός and κέλευθος could be a secondary acquisition. It is easy to see how the analogy with adjectives made most Indo-European languages drop the use of *-e/o-stems in the feminine. The opposite analogical action, however, is completely improbable: feminines in *-e/o- were ultimately eliminated in Greek and the Romance (i.e., neo-Latin) languages, as they were everywhere else, the only difference being that in the first case the elimination belongs to historical time, whereas in the second the elimination antedates the most ancient texts. Finally, the reason that Greek and Latin (and no doubt Armenian, before the loss of the notion of gender) retained Indo-European usage for a long time is perhaps this: these are the languages in which the vowel *o* remained distinct from *a;* in Indo-Iranian, Slavic, Baltic, and Germanic, *a* and *o* tended to merge, as has been seen; the distinction between masculine and feminine, then, came to be marked only by the quantity of the stem vowel, rather than by the quality of the vowel as well, as in *bonum/bonam*, φίλον/φίλᾱν, etc.; it was all the more necessary thenceforth to limit the short vowel to the masculine and the long to the feminine; the clarity of the sign of gender having diminished, the use of the sign had to become stricter in order to preserve its meaningfulness. If this explanation — which may appear tenuous, but is justified by a striking similarity — is correct, the absence of any traces of feminine *-e/o-* in Celtic would result from the comparatively rapid change of the Celtic languages before any of them were recorded, and from the very great importance assumed by the distinction between masculine and feminine. If we had Celtic texts older than the ones we do have, we would surely find feminine *-o*–stems in them.

chapter eighteen

Case-Endings with *-*bh*- and *-*m*-

THE DIFFERENCE BETWEEN A DATIVE PLURAL
with *-bh-, e.g., Skr. -bhyaḥ, Av. -byō, Lat. -bus, OOsc. -fs,
OIr. -ib, Gr. -φι(ν), and one with *-m-, e.g., Goth. -m,
OLith. -mus, OSl. -mŭ, is one of the first things to have
drawn attention to the problem of Indo-European dialectology. Since it has been established, principally by A.
Leskien, that there was no unity of Germanic, Baltic, and
Slavic postdating the period of Indo-European unity, the
very striking similarity of Germanic, Baltic, and Slavic
which we observe here cannot — granted that it is meaningful — be explained except by a dialectal distinction within
Common Indo-European.

H. Hirt (*IF,* V, 251) has supposed *-bh- to have been
originally the mark of the dative–ablative, and *-m- to
have been the mark of the instrumental, each language
having subsequently generalized one or the other. However, this is purely hypothetical, and as far as the instrumental case is concerned, the hypothesis has no support at

all.[1] Even Armenian — with only one case, the instrumental, provided by endings of this type — has only *-bh-* and no trace of *-m-:* instrumental singular *-b, -v, -w (harb, khnov, amaw)*, plural *-bkh, -vkh, -wkh (harbkh, khnovkh, amawkh)*. Armenian, then, directly contradicts Hirt's supposition. There is no trace of endings with *-m-* outside of Germanic, Baltic, and Slavic. Vedic *sánemi* is not an adverb representing a case-ending in *-mi*, and adverbs such as Lat. *partim* represent accusatives, as is indicated by the way in which *partem* is used. As for the dative, we may mention the fact that languages which elsewhere have only forms with *-m-* have the following 2nd-person dative singular pronouns: OSl. *tebĕ*, OPruss. *tebbei*, alongside Skr. *túbhya(m)*, GAv. *taibyā*, Lat. *tibī̄*, Umbr. t e f e. But personal-pronoun flection is too much in a class of its own to prove anything. The 1st-person singular pronoun has a wholly isolated form: Skr. *máhya(m)*, Arm. *inj*, Lat. *mihī̄*, Umbr. *mehe;* Armenian has the same guttural in the 2nd-person dative *khez;* and Germanic has an *-s-* which is all its own: Goth. *mis*, þus, OIce. *mér*, þér, OHG. *mir, dir*. Finally, even supposing that *-bh-* and *-m-* belonged to different cases in Indo-European, the contrast would still exist between Germanic, Baltic, and Slavic on the one hand, and Celtic, Italic, Greek, Armenian, and Indo-Iranian on the other; the contrast would have to do with the case distribution of the forms instead of a difference of origin.

This is not the only isogloss linking Germanic to Baltic and Slavic. For example, the line representing the development of *ŏ* and the line representing the fall of medial *ə* both show that these three languages arose from Indo-European dialects exhibiting certain common features. Moreover, of the two forms of the neuter collective that stands in the place of the nominative–accusative plural, viz., *-ā* and *-ə*, Slavic and Germanic generalized the first (e.g., Goth. *juka*, OSl. *jiga;* Goth. *namna*, OSl. *jimena*), while Greek generalized the second (e.g., ζυγά, ὀνόματα); however, whereas Latin generalized *-ə, (e.g., *iugă, nōmină*), Osco-Umbrian generalized *-ā (e.g., Umbr. i u k u, *vatuo,* Osc. p r ú f t ú, *comono*), as in the nominative singular of feminines with *-ā-;* the fact is not, then, really characteristic—though it is worth noting as an instance of similarity.

This noteworthy isogloss of *-m- and *-bh- is crossed by another that is related to the same endings.

In Indo-Iranian, Slavic, Baltic, and Armenian the endings in *-bh- and *-m- give rise to well-defined case-endings; thus, Skr. *-bhyaḥ and Av. *-byō mark the dative–ablative plural (the ablative almost never has an ending of its own); Skr. *-bhiḥ, GAv. *-bīš, Av. *-biš, OPers. *-biš, instrumental plural; Skr. *-bhyām, Av. *-bya (with long final: *-byā-ča) and *-byam, dative-ablative-instrumental dual (the three cases always have but one ending in the dual, which shows only a small number of distinct case-endings); Arm. *-b, -v, -w, instrumental singular, and *-bkh, -vkh, -wkh, instrumental plural; OSl. *-mi, instrumental singular, *-mi, instrumental plural, *-mŭ, dative plural, *-ma, dative-instrumental dual; Lith. *-mi, instrumental singular, *-mis, instrumental plural, *-mus, dative plural, *-ma, dative-instrumental dual; OPruss. *-mans, dative plural. All these forms are precise expressions of a certain case and a certain number.

On the contrary, the Homeric ending -φι(ν), which appears to be of Aeolian origin and is not found in the other dialects, is used for both singular and plural; it serves for all cases with "real" value, viz., dative, ablative, locative, and instrumental; it never occurs with a genitive or accusative function. Since it is a Homeric archaism, there might be some temptation to see in -φι(ν) an old form misunderstood and used indifferently to express various things. However, while the Homeric language contains many traditional archaisms and while these archaisms are used arbitrarily, at least they keep their exact value within their contexts, and nothing permits us to attribute to the Homeric language the capricious use of an old ending whose meaning has been lost. One of the outstanding characteristics of the Homeric language is precisely its extreme correctness in the use of endings that had gone out of use by the time the text transmitted was composed and fixed; the archaism of certain forms is expressed only in a lack of consistency in their use. Moreover, Lat. *-bus,* Osco-Umbr. *-fs* (*-ss, -s*) also have a multiple value: dative, ablative, locative, and instrumental; the same is true of OIr. *-ib.* Latin has, additionally, the personal pronouns *nōbīs* and *vōbīs,* but nothing can be inferred from personal-pronoun forms; moreover, these endings have the same complex value as those of ordinary nouns. It is this four-fold value of the endings with **-bh-* which permits us to account for the case synthesis that appears in Italic and Celtic; nothing else would explain this synthesis. The Latin form and the Irish form do not overlap, but they both serve for four Indo-European cases in the plural; it cannot be determined which vowel is missing in Osco-Umbrian between *f* and *s* (OOsc. -f s). As for Germanic, one form alone is attested; it may be the outcome of the synthesis of distinct forms, for various vowels could have fallen after **-m-;* but case synthesis developed, analogous to that found in Latin and Irish.

There would be grounds, then, for affirming a contrast between, first, Indo-Iranian, Slavic, Baltic, and Armenian, in which the endings with **-bh-* and **-m-* have precise values, and, secondly, Greek, Italic, Celtic, and probably Germanic, in which these same endings mark several cases —and even, in Homer, several numbers—and have the appearance of adverbs. It may be that the Eastern dialects were innovators in this respect, and that the endings in **-bh-* and **-m-* were originally adverbial forms.

The developments of the endings with **-bh-* and **-m-*

had important consequences. The Eastern dialects, in which these endings took on precise values, long preserved the cases with "real" value, viz., the locative, ablative, and instrumental; many Slavic and Baltic dialects still have the locative and the instrumental today; and Eastern Armenian still has all three cases. The Western dialects, on the other hand, show notable confusions from the start; Common Italic still had the locative, Common Germanic still had the instrumental, but neither had the three cases, and in Italic, Germanic, and Celtic we find a single form being created for all three cases. Greek, in which endings in $-\phi\iota(\nu)$ have little importance, no doubt underwent special changes that very early brought about a reduction of the declension, with retention only of the "grammatical" cases.[2]

The Eastern dialects converge at another point: Indo-Iranian, Slavic, and Baltic are the only groups showing *-su* as a locative plural ending. Armenian has a form in -s (identical to that of the accusative plural), which may have lost a final *-u. Greek has the ending -σι, which is different and which marks the plural of the dative, instrumental, and locative. The other languages have nothing corresponding to the Eastern ending *-su*.

chapter nineteen

The Genitive Plural of *-ā̄-Stems

GREEK AND ITALIC BOTH EXTEND TO ALL
*-ā̄–stems the genitive plural form of demonstrative stems
in *-ā̄-, as follows:

Hom. -άων (with -ā- maintained, because Ionic did not
have a dissyllabic form *-ηων to substitute for the early
-άων), Ion. -έων, Att. -ῶν, Dor. and Aeol.-ᾶν.

Lat. *-ārum,* Osc. -a s u m, *-azum,* Umbr. -a r u, *-arum.*
Genitives such as Lat. *caelicolum, caprigenum*[1] are found only
in a few masculines — long words in which *-um,* borrowed
from the *-o*–stems, made it possible to avoid even further
lengthening with the dissyllabic ending *-ārum.*

An extension of the same type, but of a different form,
is found in some Germanic dialects; thus, OHG. *gebōno,*
OSax. *geƀono,* OE. *giefena,* and even, once, Runic Norse
runono, but Goth. *gibo,* OIce. *gjafa.*

This concordance of Greek and Italic is very noteworthy;
the innovation is surely Common Greek and Common
Italic, and is found nowhere else. The only demonstrative

form to have been ordinarily extended to other nouns is
the nominative plural *-oi* of stems in *-o-*. But that was a
very special situation: feminine demonstrative stems in
-ā- had the same characteristic *-âs* in the nominative
plural as other nouns, while masculine stems in *-o-* had
an *-oi* which was peculiar to the demonstratives. This lack
of parallelism brought about certain analogical developments: the extension of *-oi* to the other nouns in Greek,
Latin, Irish, and Slavic, and to the adjectives in Germanic
and Baltic; the extension of *-ōs* to the demonstratives from
the other nouns in Osco-Umbrian. Nothing similar occurred for the genitive plural. The Greek and Italic innovation is unpredictable and consequently very characteristic.

Italic and Greek also tend toward innovation in the
*-ā–*stems under the influence of the *-o–*stems. Greek and
Latin re-formed the nominative plural of the *-ā–*stems on
the model of the *-o–*stems, influenced by the demonstratives: Gr. -αι, Lat. -*ae* (Osco-Umbrian naturally diverges).
As for the dative-instrumental-locative plural, Greek has
-αισι and -αις (depending on the dialects), Latin -*īs*, Oscan
-a í s, Umbrian -e s, -*er;* cf., in -*o*–stems, Gr. -οισι and -οις,
Lat. -*īs*, Osc. -ú í s, -*ois*, Umbr. -e s, -*ir*.

In the plural, then, the flection of the demonstratives
and that of the other stems in *-o-* and *-ā-* tend to become
identical in Greek and Italic. This no doubt began with the
genitive plural of *-ā–*stems, which brings out both the
antiquity and the importance of the Greco-Italic relation
shown here.

Some Observations on Vocabulary

COGNATE WORDS GENERALLY INDICATE VERY little about the relation of the languages to which they belong; there are no two languages in which a certain number of cognates could not be found. There are, nevertheless, some examples of probative value, due either to special circumstances or to the grouping of the examples.

The root **bhewə-* had the primary meaning 'grow', which is still the only meaning found in Greek (φῦσαι, φύσις, φυτόν, etc.) and Armenian (*boys* 'plant', *busanel* 'grow'). In all other Indo-European languages, the root has, at least in some of its forms, the value of the verb 'be' and complements the forms supplied by the root **es-*, i.e., present (Skr. *ásti*, Gr. ἐστι, etc.) and perfect (Skr. *ása*, Av. *åṅha*, Hom. ἦεν); hence the preterites Skr. *ábhūt*, OSl. *by, bystŭ*, Lith. *bùvo*, OIr. *ro bōi*, Lat. *fuit*. A present with **-iye-* plays an important role in the Western languages: Lat. *fīō, fīs* serves to express the idea of 'becoming'; OIr. *bīu* (3rd pers. *bīid*) is the verb of existence with a notion of duration; OE. *bīo* is synonymous with the verb *eom* (*is*), whence, through contamination of the two forms, OSax. *bium,* OHG. *bim.* To this well-defined stem of the three Western languages are related a few less clear Eastern forms: Lith. *bit(i)* 'he was', OSl. *bimĭ* (a kind of optative), Pers. *bīd* '(imp.) be'. Only Greek and Armenian remain untouched by the innovation that brought **bhewə-* together with the verb 'be'.

The root **bheudh-* kept its primary meaning 'waken' only in some of the forms of Indo-Iranian, Slavic, and Baltic; everywhere else, secondary meanings, e.g., 'pay attention to', are found; these meanings are the only ones everywhere attested for the stem **bhéudhe-*.[1] The primary meaning 'waken' must have been Common Indo-European, eventually disappearing in the Western dialects, including Greek and Armenian. This is marked by the use of words varying from one language to another to express the notion of 'wakening'; thus, Skr. *jāgarti* and Gr. ἐγείρω, Goth. *wakjan,* Lat. *vigil* and *expergiscor,* Arm. *arthun* '(p.p.) wakened', *z-arthnum* '(intrans.) I waken'.

Two cognate-groups are to be noted: Indo-Iranian and Balto-Slavic; and Italic, Celtic, and Germanic, as indicated by the following examples.

INDO-IRANIAN, SLAVIC, AND BALTIC:[2]

OSl. *(togo) radi,* cf. OPers. *(avahyā) rādiy* 'because of this'.

OSl. *slovo* 'word' and Av. *sravah-* 'word'; the coincidence of meaning is characteristic, in contrast with Gr. κλέος and Skr. *çrávaḥ* 'glory'; cf. OSl. *slava,* Lith. *szlově* 'glory'.

OSl. *bogŭ* 'god', OPers. *baga;* there is no reason to believe that the Slavic word was borrowed.

OSl. *svętŭ* 'holy', Lith. *szveñtas,* OPruss. *swints,* Av. *spəntō;* here the possibility of borrowing is excluded by the form.

OSl. *kupŭ* 'pile', OPers. *kaufa-* 'mountain'.

OSl. *kŭde* 'where', GAv. *kudā,* Skr. *kuhá* 'where'; nevertheless, cf. perhaps Umbr. *pufe,* Osc. p u f.

OSl. *samŭ* 'same', Av. *hāmō.*

OSl. *zovetŭ* 'he calls' (cf. Lith. *žavḗti*), Av. *zavaiti*, Skr. *hávate*.

OSl. *svĭtĕti* 'shine', Lith. *szvitḗti*, Skr. *çvetáḥ*, Av. *spaētō*.

OSl. *dlĭgŭ* 'long' (Serb. *dȕg;* cf. Lith. *ĭlgas*), Av. *darəɣō*, Skr. *dīrgháḥ*.

OSl. *bo* '(conj.) for', Av. *bā*.

OSl. *šuji* 'left', Av. *haoya-*, Skr. *savyáḥ;* but *lĕvŭ* is a cognate of Gr. λαιϝός, Lat. *laevus*.

OSl. *ni-čĭ* 'nothing' and *ni-čito*, Av. *naē-čiṭ;* cf. Lith. *nĕkas*.

OSl. *črŭnŭ* 'black', OPruss. *kirsnan*, Skr. *kṛṣṇaḥ*.

OSl. *griva* 'nape of the neck' (cf. Lett. *griwa* 'mouth of a river'), Av. *grīva*, Skr. *grīvá*.

OSl. *usta* 'mouth' (cf. OPruss. *austin*), Skr. *óṣṭhaḥ* 'lip'.

OSl. *vlasŭ* 'hair', Av. *varəsō*.

OSl. *-je-*, Lith. *-ja-* in compound adjectives such as Lith. *geràsis*, OSl. *dobry-jĭ, dobryjĭ;* cf. Av. *ya-*.

OSl. *bojǫ sę* 'I fear', Lith. *bijaũs*, Skr. *bháyate;* OHG. *bibēn* 'tremble' is not related to this.[3]

OSl. *javĕ avĕ* 'in evidence', Skr. *āvíḥ*, Av. *āviš*.

OSl. *gora* 'mountain' (and Lith. *girė̃* 'forest'), Skr. *giríḥ*, Av. *gairiš;* the interpretation of Gr. βορέας as 'mountain wind' is uncertain.

OSl. *(sŭ-)dravŭ* 'in good health', Av. *drva-*, OPers. *duruva-* (same meaning), and cf. Skr. *dhruváḥ* 'firm'; the characteristic fact here is that Slavic and Iranian share the meaning 'in good health'.

OSl. *ovŭ* (demonstrative), Av. *ava-;* the Avestan word provides the demonstrative of distant object with all forms except the nominative; Slavic no longer has the forms peculiar to the nominative.

Other details confirm these examples of lexical similarity, which are all the more probative in that many of them establish a particular connection between Slavic and Iranian, i.e., between Slavic and the language closest to it geographically. The stem with *-l-* in Gr. νεφέλη, Lat. *nebula*,

OIr. *nēl,* Wel. *niwl,* OHG. *nebul,* OIce. *njól* is not represented in Slavic or Baltic, but the stem in *-es-* is, as in Gr.
νέφος, Skr. *nábhah,* OSl. *nebo,* Lith. *debesìs.* It is true, on the
other hand, that we find Lith. *miglà,* OSl. *mŭgla-* together
with Gr.ὀμίχλη 'cloud'. The proper name for 'honey', i.e.,
Gr. μέλι, Lat. *mel,* OIr. *mil,* Goth. *miliþ,* Arm. *melr* (the last
influenced no doubt by **medhu*), is not represented in
either Slavic or Indo-Iranian.

(Add.) To the terms which Slavic and Indo-Iranian, but
particularly Iranian, have in common, we must add the
verb meaning 'write'. The verb is not found throughout
Iranian. It is well attested in Old Persian, where we find
the infinitive *nip(a)ištanaiy* 'write', the aorist *niyapišam* 'I
wrote', and the verbal adjective *nipištam* 'written', but it is
wanting in the Avesta. It is found in Ossetic: *finsun* 'write',
and the Sogdian word *np'ys'kw* 'who writes', which occurs in
the *Sutra of Causes and Effects* (1. 533), does not appear to
be a borrowing from Persian; the term is, then, both
Persian and Scythian. We know that, with the meaning
'write', the root also occurs in Slavic (OSl. *pišǫ, pĭsati*) and
Old Prussian (*peisāton* 'written', *peisai* 'he writes', *popeisauns*
'written on, [G.] beschrieben'), but nowhere else. The case
is comparable to that of OSl. *slovo,* which corresponds in
form to Skr. *çrávah,* Gr. κλέ(ϝ)ος, but whose meaning is
duplicated only in Av. *sravō* 'word'. Another notable semantic phenomenon is the coexistence of the meanings
'share, wealth' and 'god' in II. *bhaga-* and OSl. *bogo-* (*bogŭ,
ubogŭ, bogatŭ,* etc.). In Indo-Iranian, Baltic, and Slavic per-
sists the vocabulary of a single segment of Indo-European
civilization.

It is no accident that the words for 'thunder' and 'god of
thunder' should be clearly related: Ved. *parjányah,* OSl.
perunŭ, Lith. *perkúnas,* OPruss. *percunis* (Voc.). Nor is it
an accident that the "animate" word for 'water', II. *ap-,*
should not have any cognates outside of Baltic, i.e., apart

from OPruss. *ape* '(LG.) vlys' (Voc.), Lith. *ùpè* 'stream'; Gr. *ὀπός* 'sap' is related in meaning to OSl. *sokŭ*, etc. The Old Slavic word for 'shame', *sramŭ* (Russ. *sórom*, Pol. *srom*) has no cognate outside of Iranian, i.e., apart from Av. *fšarma-*, Pers. *šarm*, Sogd. *sβ'rm* (= *šfarm*, with *fš-* metathesized to *šf-*). The pejorative particle in Serb. *kä-vrān*, etc., has no cognate outside of Iranian.[4]

There are many other cognate words in Indo-Iranian, Slavic, and Baltic.

Thus, while Gr. *αἶξ* (*αἰγός*) goes with Arm. *ayc* 'she-goat', Lith. *ožỹs* 'he-goat', *oškà* 'she-goat', and OPruss, *wosee* 'she-goat' (Voc.) (cf. OSl. *azino* 'skin, hide', in normal alternation with Skr. *ajáḥ* 'he-goat'), Ir. *ag* is a separate word.[5] Nevertheless, Av. *izaēna-* 'made of leather' is related to Gr. *αἶξ* except for the prothetic *a-*, the absence of which is normal in Indo-Iranian.

The *m* of Lat. *spūma, pūmex* is found as well in OHG. *feim*, OE. *fām*, while the *n* of Skr. *phénaḥ* 'foam' is the same as the *n* of OSl. *pěna*, OPruss. *spoayno*, Lith. *spáinė*.

Sanskrit *bahíḥ* 'outside' is related only to OSl. *bes, bez* 'without', Lett *bez*, Lith. and OPruss. *be*. As for the meaning, cf. Skr. *āvíḥ*, GAv. *āviš*, together with OSl. *avě*.

In the West, we find the meaning 'wooded area' in Lat. *lūcus* (OLat. *loucom*, accus.), Osc. l ú v k e í (locative), OHG. *lōh*, OE. *lēah*, OIce. *lō*. In the East, the meaning of Skr. *lokáḥ*, Lith. *laũkas*, OPruss. *laucks* is 'clearing'; in Baltic, this word takes the place of the original **agro-* 'field', which disappeared from Baltic and Slavic.

The Baltic words for 'milk' are curious. Alongside Ved. *páyaḥ*, Av. *payō* and Av. *paēma*, Pahl. *pēm*, Lithuanian has *pěnas;* alongside Ved. *dádhi* (gen. *dadhnáḥ*), Old Prussian has *dadan* (Voc., neuter). The exactness of these relations is striking in view of the aberrant forms found in the Western dialects, e.g., Gr. *γάλα*, Lat. *lac*.

The stem **prǝwo-* 'first' is attested only in Indo-Iranian (Skr. *púrvaḥ*, etc.) and Slavic (OSl. *prŭvŭ*, etc.); it is not found anywhere else; Baltic has a closely related form, i.e., Lith. *pìrmas,* OPruss. *pirmas.* The similarity of Skr. *aṣṭamáḥ* 'eighth', Av. *aštəmō* to Lith. *ãšmas,* OPruss. *asman,* and OSl. *osmŭ* is curious, although Irish also has *ochtmad.* Like *nōmad* 'ninth' in comparison with Lat. *nōnus,* the form is recent. The Italo-Celtic form of the ordinal 'eighth' should have been of the type of Lat. *octāvus* (cf. Gr. *ὄγδοος*). Forms such as Skr. *aṣṭamáḥ* and OSl. *osmŭ* show the influence of the word for the preceding number: Skr. *saptamáḥ,* Pers. *haftum* (cf. Lat. *septimus*) and OPruss. *sepmas,* Lith. *sẽkmas,* OSl. *sedmŭ,* Gr. *ἕβδομος.*

For Ved. *yáti* 'he rides', which is common in Indic and barely represented in Iranian (Av. *yāiti?*), Slavic has *ĕdǫ, jaxati* and Lithuanian has *jóju, jóti,* which have the same meaning. Whatever may be the explanation of the *ĕ*–vocalism of the Slavic present, it is clear that OSl. *ĕdǫ* has the same relation to the Vedic stem *yā-* that Sl. **jĭdǫ* has to the Vedic stem *e-/i-;* cf. Gr. *εἶμι.* The Lithuanian derivative *jóju* is similarly a substitute for an athematic form **yā-mi.* This root occurs nowhere else. (We might cite, at most, an Irish noun *āth* 'ford'; the connection is doubtful, however, and it does not appear in H. Pedersen's *Vergleichende Grammatik.*) For the same notion, Celtic and Germanic have another word: OHG. *rītan,* OIr. *riad,* Gaul. *rēda.*

Old Prussian *girtwei* 'to praise' and Lith. *giriù, gìrti* 'to praise' are very close to Ved. *gṛṇấti* 'he sings (of), celebrates', *gī́r* 'song (of praise for a god)' (accus. *gíram*), Av. *gərənte* 'they praise, celebrate', GAv. *garō* (acc. pl.) 'songs of praise'. Even if Lat. *grātus, grātia* and Gr. *γέρας,* Ir. *grād* 'love', and Osc. *brateis* '(Lat.) gratiis' are related, their sense is quite different.

The more closely we examine these lexical correspondences, the more clearly emerges the close relation of the Indo-Iranian, Baltic, and Slavic vocabularies. For example, the root **dhegʷh-* 'burn' is found even in Celtic (Ir. *daig* 'fire') and Latin (*foveō*), but we find exact cognates of Skr. *dáhati* only in Lith. *degù* and OSl. *žegǫ* (with a secondary change); cf. Alb. *djek*. Likewise, Lat. *palea* is related to Skr. *palāvaḥ*, but only in OSl. *plěva* (Ruthenian *polóva*), OPruss. *pelwo*, Lett. *pelus*, etc., do we recognize the element -*w*- of the Sanskrit word.

The root **teus*- is perhaps to be seen in Germanic and Celtic,[6] but occurrences there show no connection as complete as the one between OPruss. *tusnan* 'still, (G.) still' and Skr. *tuṣṇím*, Av. *tušniš*, or between Pol. *po-tuszyć* and Av. *taošayeiti*, or between OSl. *tŭštŭ* and Skr. *tucchyáḥ*. Even OPruss. *tussīse*-, from **tusē*-, is exactly what we should have expected for Skr. *tuṣyáti*.

GERMANIC, CELTIC, AND ITALIC:

In addition to the words which these three languages possess in common with Slavic and Baltic, there are words which are not found elsewhere. Following are a few striking examples:[7]

Lat. *piscis*, OIr. *īasc*, Goth. *fisks*. The Central Indo-European area has another word: Gr. ἰχθῦς, Arm. *jukn*, Lith. *žuvìs*, OPruss. *suckis, suckans;* the other languages have their own words.

Lat. *vātēs*, OIr. *fáith* 'poet', OHG. *wuot* 'frenzy', OIce. *óðr* 'poetry'.

Lat. *flōs*, OIr. *blāth*, OHG. *bluomo* and *bluot*.

Lat. *caecus* 'blind', and Ir. *caech*, Goth. *haihs* 'blind in one eye'; very few nouns designating physical disabilities are common to more than one language in the Indo-European family.

Lat. *vāstus*, OIr. *fās*, OHG. *wuosti*.

Lat. *crībrum*, OIr. *criathar*, OE. *hridder*. Gr. κρίνω is of the same word family, but does not have the technical meaning 'I sift'; on the other hand, Goth. *hrains* 'pure' no doubt meant 'sifted' originally.

Lat. *porca*, OIr. *rech*, OHG. *furuh* 'furrow'. Arm. *herk* 'land that has been cleared and tilled' does not belong to this group, for the *k* can represent only **g;* cf. perhaps *harkanel* 'break'.

Lat. *hasta,* Ir. *gat* 'willow twig', Goth. *gazds* 'goad'.

Lat. *caper,* Wel. *caer-,* OIce. *hafr* 'he-goat'; Gr. κάπρος 'boar', like Pers. *čapiš,* etc., is not related to this word, because of the meaning.

Lat. *capiō,* Goth. *hafja;* Lat. *captō,* OIr. *cachtaim,* OSax. *haftōn.* The formation indicates a connection between Lat. *capiō* and OIr. *gaibim,* whose root is found in Lat. *habēre* (formed like Goth. *haban*), Osc. *hafiest* 'he will have'.

Lat. *alō,* OIr. *alim,* Goth. *ala;* elsewhere, there are only traces of the root, as in Gr. ἄν-αλτος.

Lat. *plānus,* Gaul. *(Medio-)lānum;* OIr. *lār* 'ground', OE. *flōr.*

Lat. *manus,* Umbr. m a n f (acc. pl.), Osc. *manim* (acc. sing.), OIce. and OE. *mund;* cf. MBret. *malazn* 'sheaf'[8] in contrast to (1) expression by means of the root **gher-* in Gr.χείρ, Alb. *dorε,* Arm. *jeřn* 'hand', (2) Skr. *hástaḥ* = OPers. *dasta* and (3) OSl. *rǫka.*

Lat. *mālus* 'mast', ModIr. *maide* 'stick', Ir. *matan* (with *t* representing the voiced stop *d*) 'club', *admat,*[9] OHG. *mast* 'pole', OIce. *mastr* 'mast'.

Lat. *mentum* 'chin', Wel. *mant* 'jaw', Goth. *munþs,* OHG. *mund* 'mouth'.

Lat. *natrix,* Ir. *nathir* (gen. *nathrach*), OIce. *naðr.*

There are also many Celto-Germanic and Italo-Germanic cognates; the words thus attested may be wanting only by chance in Italic or in Celtic. There is no proof even that certain of the lexical correspondences noted above between Celtic and Italic do not come from the Germano-Celto-Italic inventory of words. The three languages have notably similar vocabularies.

(Add.) It would certainly be profitable to undertake a geographical examination of the vocabulary of Indo-European. P. Kretschmer has already indicated as much in his *Einleitung gr. Spr.* A few examples will show the interest of a systematic undertaking of such a project.

From the root *sneig^wh*- 'to snow', there is an athematic root noun in the Greek accusative νίφα (Hesiod) — with several Homeric derivatives — in Lat. *nix, nivem* and in Wel. *nyf;* and there is a thematic form in OSl. *sněgŭ,* Lith. *sněgas,* OPruss. *snaygis,* Goth. *snaiws.* The corresponding present is thematic in Av. *snaēžaiti,* Lith. *sněga,* Gr. νείφει, OLat. *nīvit* (in a verse by Pacuvius), OHG. *snīwit.* There is also a present with nasal infix: Lith. *sniñga,* Lat. *ninguit.* Here we see a tie between Germanic and Slavic.

It is surely no accident that 'man' should be a 'mortal' in Sanskrit (*mártaḥ, mártyaḥ*), Iranian (Av. *mašyō,* etc.), Armenian (*mard*), and Greek (μορτός, βροτός), whereas the notion of 'earthly being' prevails in Lithuanian (*žmŭ̃*), Germanic (Goth. *guma,* etc.), and Celtic (Ir. *duine*[10]). Greek agrees here with the Eastern dialects, and Baltic with the Western dialects.

It is surely no accident, either, that the word for 'citadel' should be attested in Sanskrit (*pūḥ,* acc. sing. *púram*), Lithuanian (*pilìs*), and Greek (πόλις, πτόλις), but not be found anywhere else. But the simple absence of a word proves little. Nevertheless, there is no lack of such lexical limitations. Thus we do not find, either, outside of Indo-Iranian, Baltic, and Greek, the root of Skr. *arghāḥ* 'value, recompense', Lith. *algà,* Gr. ἀλφή.

Elsewhere, Indo-Iranian, Armenian, and Greek concord, as in Skr. *járati* 'he grows old', Arm. *cer* 'old', Gr. γέρων. For the word meaning 'cloud' — Skr. *meghāḥ,* Arm. *mēg,* and Gr. ὀμιχλή, OSl. *mĭgla,* Lith. *miglà* — there are as many as four groups, with a curious distribution of forms.

A significant type of distribution is that of the words for 'lamb'. There are two of them. One is found only in Indo-Iranian, Armenian, and Greek: Skr. *úraṇaḥ,* Pers. *barra,* Arm. *garn,* Gr. ϝαρήν. The other, Gr. ἀμνός, Lat. *agnus,* includes Celtic and Germanic, and extends even to Slavic: *agnĭci, agne.* The intermediate position of Greek, in which Eastern and Western elements coexist, is striking.

Conclusion

THE PHENOMENA JUST STUDIED SHOW THAT the principal lines of demarcation in the Indo-European family pass between the Eastern dialects on the one hand and the Western dialects on the other.

Indo-Iranian, Slavic, Baltic, and Armenian (together with Albanian) constitute the Eastern group, which shows several common characteristics, viz., a guttural development covering various phenomena, a tendency to shift from *s to š (and from *z to ž) under certain conditions, and the use of endings in *bh (or *m) with precise number and case value. These various features almost surely result from innovations and consequently attest a significant period of common development. This does not mean that the dialect group was indivisible, or that the phenomena studied were brought about by imitation; what confronts us, rather, is a series of independently realized innovations, as is indicated by detailed examination of the facts. Thus we observe that the Indo-Iranian, Albanian, Baltic, and Slavic fusion of *ă and *ŏ extends to Germanic on the one hand, but on the other hand does not take place in Armenian; the fall of medial *∂ occurs throughout the Eastern area and even in Germanic, but is not found in Sanskrit; the development *-euye- is Iranian, Slavic, and Baltic and no doubt also Germanic, but Sanskrit and Armenian show *-ewye-, as do Greek, Italic, and Celtic. The vocabularies of Indo-Iranian, Baltic, and Slavic show numerous cognates. The Eastern dialects thus constitute a natural group.

The Western group—Germanic, Celtic, and Italic—is no less natural, presenting certain highly characteristic common features, viz., the development of -ss- from *-tt-, a perfect often occurring without reduplication, formation of the preterite through a combination of the perfect and the aorist, an alternation of *-yo- and *-ĭ- in the suffix of the derived present, the rarity of the type λόγος, use of the suffix *-tūt-, and cognate words. In addition, certain features which are found elsewhere are common to Germanic, Celtic, and Italic, viz., guttural development (in common with Greek), absence of the augment (in common with Baltic and Slavic), use of endings with *-bh- (or *-m-) for the dative, ablative, locative, and instrumental, and fusion of aspirated and non-aspirated voiceless stops (in common with Baltic, Slavic, and, in part, Greek).

As we have seen, however, one of the three Western languages, Germanic, coincides at several points with the Eastern group; we might add to these the form of certain personal pronouns, especially the 1st and 2nd persons dual and plural. Additionally, Germanic resembles Baltic and Slavic in the use of endings in *-m-, rather than *-bh-; also to be noted is the fact that the numerals 'twenty', 'thirty', etc., are expressed by a juxtaposition of 'two', 'three', etc., and the word signifying 'group of ten', rather than by shortened forms of the type Gr. ϝίκατι, εἴκοσι, Lat. vīgintī, Arm. khsan; Gr. τριάκοντα, Lat. trīgintā, Arm. eresun, etc.

At the same time, another of the three Western languages, Italic, shows certain special areas of similarity with

Greek: unvoicing of the voiced aspirated stops, and borrowing of the genitive plural of *-ā–stems from the demonstrative flection. These are very early, important innovations not found anywhere else. Greek and Italic, along with prehistoric Armenian, are the only languages that preserve feminine gender in *-o–stem nouns. There may also be convergence in the matter of preverb accent;[1] in this matter, Greek is completely at variance with Sanskrit and we find the trace of a dialectal syntactic phenomenon.[2] H. Hirt (*IF,* XVII, 395) has also tried to demonstrate the identity of certain Greek and Latin infinitives. However, cognate words are of negligible importance; they are few in number, and these few (e.g., Gr. ἅλλομαι and Lat. *saliō*) are not striking in their meaning.

All this does not prevent Greek from being linked in other areas with languages of the Eastern group. The Greek change of *s to *h* also occurs in Armenian and Iranian. The vowel developed before vocalic sonants, especially when nasal, is *a* (as in Armenian and Indo-Iranian). There is always a prothetic vowel before initial *r*—except that Greek does not place a vowel before any *ρ* introduced at a late date (the case of *sr* and *wr* particularly), whereas Armenian shows no such distinction. The use of the suffix *-tero-* in the formation of the secondary comparatives recurs only in Indo-Iranian. The augment is preserved, as it is in Armenian and Indo-Iranian. The secondary present suffix, as well as the suffix of verbs of state, has the form *-ye/yo-,* as in Indo-Iranian. From several points of view, then, Greek shows correspondences with Armenian and Indo-Iranian. With Baltic and Slavic it has in common the total synthesis of the genitive and ablative, as well as a few lexical features.

Greek, then, occupies a position midway between Italic and the Eastern languages, i.e., Armenian and Indo-Iranian, but particularly Iranian. It stems from a group of Indo-European idioms within which many isoglosses came to intersect.

Among the Eastern languages, Armenian—which keeps the distinction between *$\check{a}$ and *$\check{o}$, and *$\bar{a}$ and *$\bar{o}$—is relatively close to the Western group. On the other hand, there are some special points of contact with Slavic and Baltic, particularly in the present suffixes *-*ye/yo*- and *-*ĭ̆*- and in the role of the suffix *-*lo*-. A consonant shift comparable to that of Germanic would seem to be an important fact but, as we have seen, it does not establish a valid point of contact.

The respective situation of the Indo-European dialects may be schematized as follows, with the various Indo-European idioms given the same names as the historically attested languages that grew from them:

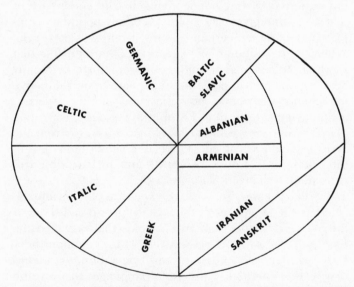

This very rough diagram, which omits languages that are not attested by a sustained textual tradition, does not correspond to any particular historical phenomenon. It has linguistic value only and indicates what we may suppose to have been the respective situation of the Indo-

European dialects before the period when each of the languages, taking root in new territory, became isolated and ceased to develop in common with its neighbors. The amount of space given to each idiom in the diagram is purely arbitrary; it is possible that an Indo-European language spoken at the beginning of historical time over a very vast area was based upon a quite small number of Indo-European idioms, and vice versa. The linguistic phenomena studied here lead only to linguistic conclusions, and the diagram expressing these conclusions has meaning only for linguists.

One observation must be made, however. The Indo-European idioms occupied an area in which linguistic innovations occurred independently in contiguous parts of that area, though nowhere was there any boundary completely separating certain groups from certain others. When the separation took place, no doubt gradually — that is, when colonists and conquerors went forth to occupy new regions and impose their language upon the native inhabitants — there was no dislocation in the respective arrangement of the Indo-European languages; what took place, rather, was a radial movement outward from the area originally occupied. There is no indication that in the course of that outward growth any of the Indo-European idioms changed places with each other.

We do not know, and we have no means of determining, whether the languages of the Eastern group and those of the Western group stem from idioms that occupied the East and West sections, respectively, of the common Indo-European territory. But, with this reservation, the idioms that were contiguous gave rise to languages that are still appreciably the most similar in the historical period. There is no proof that what occurred in Indo-European parallels what occurred later in Germanic when the Gothic dialects, relatively close to the Scandinavian dialects, came to be wholly separated from them and were dispersed over a wide area. If there had been such an occurrence, it would no doubt have had the same result as the situation involving Gothic: with the speakers of Gothic so dispersed, the language completely disappeared after a few centuries. And nothing could be more natural, for the groups that are most adventurous and allow themselves to be drawn farthest away from the mass of speakers of their language are the ones that are most open to absorption by other peoples and to the loss of their own idiom. The dispersion of the Indo-European languages is quite similar to that of the Slavic languages: it would be easy to cover the territory of Slavic with isoglosses like those drawn for Indo-European, and they would show that the Slavic dialects expanded—a few, like Russian, on a vast scale—but without any change in their respective positions.

Another conclusion, more important from the linguistic point of view, is that even before the separation Indo-European was composed of idioms which were already highly differentiated, and that we have no right to view Indo-European as a single language. The characteristic features of each of the large groups (Slavic, Germanic, Baltic, etc.) mark, to a great extent, the continuation of phenomena that do not belong to Indo-European in general and yet do belong to the Indo-European period. Some groups, such as Indo-Iranian and Italo-Celtic, even include representatives of distinct Indo-European dialects. Consideration of such dialectal distinctions, which must never be neglected, will add complexity—but precision as well—to the comparative study of the grammar of the Indo-European languages.

Notes

AUTHOR'S FOREWORD
1. See W. Streitberg, *Gotisches Elementarbuch,* 5th and 6th eds. (Heidelberg, 1920), par. 117, p. 91.

INTRODUCTION
1. See Louis Gauchat, "L'Unité phonétique dans le patois d'une commune", in *Aus romanischen Sprachen und Literaturen, Festschrift Heinrich Morf* (Halle, 1905), pp. 175–232.
2. *Essai de méthodologie linguistique dans le domaine des langues et des patois romans.* Paris, 1906.
3. The principle involved here (originally formulated in the case of the Romance languages by H. Schuchardt) was published for the first time by J. Schmidt in his *Verwandtschaftsverhältnisse der indogermanischen Sprachen* (Weimar, 1872); this was the famous wave theory. K. Brugmann dis-

cussed the problem in 1884 in the *Internationale Zeitschrift für allgemeine Sprachwissenschaft* (I, 226), as did P. Kretschmer in his *Einleitung in die Geschichte der griechischen Sprache* (Göttingen, 1896), p. 93ff. (This work will hereafter be cited as *Einleitung gr. Spr.*) The current state of the question and bibliography are given in O. Schrader, *Sprachvergleichung und Urgeschichte,* 3rd ed. (Jena, 1906–07), p. 53ff., and H. Hirt, *Die Indogermanen, ihre Verbreitung, ihre Urheimat und ihre Kultur* (Strasbourg, 1905–07), p. 89ff. and p. 579ff. (This work will hereafter be cited as *Indogermanen.*) See, too, E. Hermann, "Über das Rekonstruieren", *KZ,* XLI, 1.

4. The hypothesis of P. G. Goidanich — *L'Origine e le forme della dittongazione romanza, Zeitschrift für romanische Philologie,* Beiheft 5 (Halle, 1907) — brings no change to the fundamental fact that the diphthong is recent, and that is the only fact to be considered here.

5. This has been shown particularly by Solmsen in a series of articles in volumes LVIII through LXII of the *Rheinisches Museum für Philologie.*

CHAPTER I

1. *Vergleichendes Wörterbuch der indogermanischen Sprachen.* 4th ed. Göttingen, 1890.

2. See W. Stokes and A. Bezzenberger, *Wortschatz der keltischen Einheit, Urkeltischer Sprachschatz* (Göttingen, 1894), p.88. This work forms Part II of Fick, op. cit. (previous note).

3. For Celtic, see W. Stokes, *KZ,* XL, 249.

4. See *verbum* in A. Walde, *Lateinisches etymologisches Wörterbuch,* 2nd ed. (Heidelberg, 1910).

CHAPTER II

1. See C. Bartholomae, *IF,* XIX, Beiheft, 108.

CHAPTER III

1. See Julien Havet, *Revue celtique,* XXVIII, 113.

2. Most of these examples have already appeared in Meillet, *De indo-europaea radice* *men- '*mente agitare*' (Paris, 1897) and H. Hirt, *IF,* XXI, 167.

3. See A. Leskien, "Bildung der Nomina im Litauischen", *Abhandlungen der philologisch-historichen Classe der königlichen sächsischen Akademie der Wissenschaften,* XII, 498. This article will be cited hereafter as "Bildung".

4. See the Thessalian hypothesis of J. Schmidt (*KZ,* XXXVIII, 29) and P. Kretschmer's objections (*Glotta,* I, 58).

5. For the forms, see G. Dottin, *Les Désinences verbales en -r en sanskrit, en italique et en celtique* (Rennes, 1896).

6. See H. Pedersen, *KZ,* XL, 170.

7. For Irish, see J. Vendryes, *Grammaire du vieil irlandais* (Paris, 1908), par. 331, p. 173. This work will hereafter be cited as *Gram. v. irl.*

8. Ibid., par. 332, p. 173 and par. 336, p. 176.

9. See J. Vendryes, *MSL,* XIII, 384.

10. The words in other languages that have been related to these—such as those given by E. Lidén (*IF,* XIX, 325)—do not have exactly the same meaning or form.

11. See K. Brugmann, "Demonstrativ-Pronomina", *Abhandlungen der philologisch-historischen Classe der königlichen sächsischen Akademie der Wissenschaften,* XXII, 83.

12. See Vendryes, *Gram. v. irl.,* par. 400, p. 210.

CHAPTER IV

1. See W. Schulze, *Zur Geschichte lateinischer Eigennamen,* Königliche Gesellschaft der Wissenschaften zu Göttingen, Philologisch–historische Klasse, N.S., V, No. 5 (Berlin, 1904), p. 520, and K. Brugmann, *IF,* XXII, 191.

2. See R. Trautmann, *Germanische Lautgesetze* (Kirchhain N.-L., 1906), p. 62.

3. *Vergleichende slavische Grammatik* (Göttingen, 1906–08), I, 206, n. 1.

4. *Izvěstija otdělenja russkago jazyka i slovesnoti imp. akad. nauk,* VI, No. 1, 229.

5. Ibid., XI, No. 1, 269.

6. See Leskien, "Bildung", p. 317. Juškevič accents *éldija,* which is surprising; the words are related, but not identical: let us note the absence of the Common Indo-European word **nāw-* in both the Baltic and the Slavic groups.

7. *(Add.)* This chapter has been discussed several times, and in detail, first by Porzezinski (*Rocznik slawistyczny,* IV, 1) and J. Endzelin *(Salviano-baltiiskie etiudy* [Kharkov, 1911]), and then by J. Rozwadowski (*Rocznik slaw.,* V, 1). The reader is referred to their studies. Endzelin and Rozwadowski, while criticizing some of the details of the views presented here and presenting many new views of their own, arrive nevertheless at similar conclusions. Slavic and Baltic are surely very closely related to each other. The noun flections in particular are similar. There are, however, some important differences, especially in the verbal systems. (See Mladenov, *Revue des études slaves,* II, 38.) Moreover, there is no decisive proof that there was ever a Balto-Slavic national unity comparable to the unity of Indic and Iranian. On the contrary, linguistic developments indicate the diffuse and almost imperceptible unity of tribes living close to each other and under like conditions. N. van Wijk, studying the effects of Saussure's law in Slavic, has arrived at conclusions similar to mine concerning the independence of accent shift in Slavic and in Baltic; see *IF,* XL, 1.

CHAPTER V

1. See Meillet, *Journal asiatique,* XIX, 562.

2. See H. Osthoff, *IF,* IV, 281.

CHAPTER VI

1. See Meillet, *MSL,* IX, 142; XI, 11; XIII, 250; XIV, 190.

2. See Eulenburg, *IF,* XVI, 35 and the bibliography presented there.

3. See H. Osthoff, *Etymologisches Parerga* (Leipzig, 1901), p. 323.

CHAPTER VII

1. For Albanian, see Pedersen, *KZ,* XXXIX, 429. For Illyrian, see Johansson, *IF,* XIV, 267; for Thracian and Phrygian, ibid., 269.

CHAPTER VIII

1. For the forms of this word, see H. Osthoff, *IF,* XX, 177, and the bibliographical references contained therein. For examples of the fall of *ǝ* in Germanic, see H. Hirt, *Der indogermanische Ablaut, vornehmlich in seinem Verhältnis zur Betonung* (Strasbourg, 1900), par. 146. The latter work will be cited hereafter as *Ablaut.*

2. See H. Hübschmann, *IF, Anzeiger für indogermanische Sprach- und Altertumskunde,* X, 45.

3. See Saussure, op. cit. (above, p. 84), p. 242.

4. This form occurs in the Rig-Veda in I, 11, 2; I, 66, 3; IV, 20, 5; V, 25, 5; VIII, 99, 7; IX, 90, 3.

5. *Altindische Grammatik,* I (Göttingen, 1896), par. 48b, p. 53.

6. See the examples cited in Arnold, *Vedic Metre in its Historical Development* (Cambridge, 1905), p. 91.

7. *Recueil de mémoires de philologie classique et d'archéologie offerts à Jules Nicole* (Geneva, 1905), p. 511, n. 2.

8. See W. Prellwitz, *Etymologisches Wörterbuch der griechischen Sprache,* 2nd ed. (Göttingen, 1905), under this word.

9. See K. Brugmann, *Grundriss der vergleichenden Grammatik der indogermanischen Sprachen,* 2nd ed. (Strasbourg, 1897), I, 477, par. 527, and *Griechische Grammatik,* 3rd ed. (Munich, 1900), p. 88. The former work will hereafter be cited as *Grundriss.*

CHAPTER IX

1. See H. Hübschmann, *Armenische Grammatik* (Leipzig, 1895), p. 414. This work will be cited hereafter as *Arm. Gram.*

2. See Meillet, *Introduction à l'étude comparative des langues indo-européennes,* 2nd ed. (Paris, 1907), p. 102; 8th ed. (Paris, 1937, reprinted 1964, University of Alabama Press, University, Ala.), p. 129.

3. *(Add.)* For the development of *-wy-* in Celtic, see H. Pedersen, *Vergleichende Grammatik der keltischen Sprachen* (Göttingen, 1908–09), I, 55.

CHAPTER X

1. *Beiträge zur Geschichte der deutschen Sprache und Literatur,* I, 199, and "Vorgeschichte der altgermanischen Dialekte", *Grundriss der germanischen Philologie,* ed. H. Paul, 2nd ed. (Strasbourg, 1897), I, 367.

2. See Carl Meinhof, *Grundriss einer Lautlehre der Bantusprachen* (Leipzig, 1899).

3. *Parole,* IX, 124, and *Classification des dialectes arméniens,* Bibliothèque de l'Ecole Pratique des Hautes Etudes, Sciences historiques et philologiques, No. 173 (Paris, 1909), p. 3 et passim.

4. *Parole,* IX, 132.

5. See H. Pedersen, *Philologica,* I, 45.

CHAPTER XI

1. For the shift from *kh* to *x* in Armenian and Slavic, see H. Pedersen, *KZ,* XL, 173.

2. See, for example, Strekelj, *Archiv für slavische Philologie,* XXVIII, 488.

3. See Meillet, *Etudes sur l'étymologie et le vocabulaire du vieux slave* (Paris, 1902–05), p. 174.

4. See O. Lagerkrantz, *Zur griechischen Lautgeschichte* (Uppsala, 1898), p. 69.

5. See V. Miller, *Die Sprache der Osseten* (Strasbourg, 1903), p. 30. This work supplements W. Geiger and E. Kuhn, eds., *Grundriss der iranischen Philologie*, I (Strasbourg, 1895–1901).

6. See Walde, *Lat. etym. Wört.*, under "mamphur".

CHAPTER XII

1. Several scholars have observed a shift in Iranian from *št* to *st*, but its dialectal conditions are not known. See H. Hübschmann, *Persische Studien* (Strasbourg, 1895), p. 236, par. 130, and the contributions of Salemann and Horn in W. Geiger and E. Kuhn, eds., *Grundriss der iranischen Philologie*, I (Strasbourg, 1895–1901), part 1, p. 262; part 2, p. 86.

2. See Meillet, *MSL*, XIV, 412.

3. See Brugmann, *Grundriss*, p. 727, par. 818, n.2.

4. See E. Berneker, *Die preussische Sprache, Texte, Grammatik, etymologisches Worterbuch* (Strasbourg, 1896), p. 167.

5. In the *Sitzungsberichte* of the Berlin Academy, I (1908), 16, E. Meyer mentions the *nāsatya* among the Indo-Iranian gods worshipped by the king of Mitani (fourteenth century B.C.). If, as Meyer believes, the word is to be understood as Iranian, the shift from intervocalic *s* to *h* would be a relatively recent phenomenon. However, given a date so much earlier than the date of attestation of the Iranians, nothing proves that these gods were indeed Iranian gods. They may have been gods of Aryans other than the Iranians—of the Aryans who were later to migrate to India, for example, or perhaps of other Aryan peoples about whom nothing is known.

6. See A. Thumb, *Untersuchungen über den Spiritus asper im Griechischen* (Strasbourg, 1888), passim.

7. See Meillet, *MSL*, XIV, 163.

8. See Meillet, *MSL*, XXI, 211.

CHAPTER XIII

1. See H. Pedersen, *KZ*, XXXIX, 336.

2. See Meillet, *IF*, X, 63.

3. For the development of *d* from IE. **t* in Arm. *da, du,* see Meillet, *MSL*, XV, 91.

4. For the physiological principle underlying these developments, see Meillet, *IF, Anzeiger für indogermanische Sprach- und Altertumskunde,* XV, 216.

5. See Kretschmer, *Einleitung,* p. 208, and Hirt, *Indogermanen,* p. 600.

6. See Hempl, *Journal für germanische Philologie,* IV, 70.

7. See J.-P. Rousselot, *Principes de phonétique expérimentale,* I (Paris, 1897–1901), 497, for a description of this development.

8. See the outline of H. Adjarian's studies in *Parole,* IX, 119, and the analysis thereof in Rousselot, op. cit. (above, note 7), p. 502.

CHAPTER XIV

1. This has been shown by J. Wackernagel, "Wortumfang und Wortform", *Nachrichten* of the Göttingen Academy (1906), 147.

2. See W. Geiger, *Grundriss der iranischen Philologie,* I (Strasbourg, 1895–1901), part 2, p. 340.

3. See R. Trautmann, *Germanische Lautgesetze* (Kirchhain N.-L., 1906), p. 48.

4. See Meillet, *Revue celtique,* XXVII, 369.

CHAPTER XV

1. For this form and a few others, see K. Brugmann, *Grundriss der vergleichenden Grammatik der indogermanischen Sprachen,* II (Strasbourg, 1888–92), 1212.

2. See W. D. Whitney, *A Sanskrit Grammar* (Leipzig, 1879), par. 790 *b* and *c.*

3. See the lists of strong verbs in Vendryes, *Gram. v. irl.,* par. 400, p. 210.

CHAPTER XVI

1. See Meillet, *MSL,* XI, 297.

2. For this item and the last but one, see E. Lidén, *Blandade språkhistorika bidrag,* I (Göteborg, 1903).

3. See W. Streitberg, *Urgermanische Grammatik* (Heidelberg, 1896), par. 206, esp. p. 305.

4. See C. D. Buck, *A Grammar of Oscan and Umbrian* (Boston, 1904), par. 216, p. 165.

5. *(Add.)* Albanian—unfortunately neglected in the foregoing chapter—stands with Germanic and Italo-Celtic as far as the verb is concerned. See H. Pedersen, *KZ,* XXXVI, 323; Meillet, *MSL,* XIX, 119; Jokl, *IF,* XXXVII, 105. As for the noun, the situation is quite different: there was apparently no suffix *-ĭ- alternating with *-ye/yo-.

CHAPTER XVII

1. See K. Brugmann, *Grundriss der vergleichenden Grammatik der indogermanischen Sprachen,* II, 2nd ed. (Strasbourg, 1906–16), part 1, p. 367.

2. See Ernault, *Zeitschrift für celtische Philologie,* II, 513.

3. See Meillet, *MSL,* XIII, 213.

4. See K. Brugmann, *Abhandlungen der philologisch-historischen Classe der königlichen sächsischen Akademie der Wissenschaften,* XXV, No. 5, 72.

5. Ibid., p. 28.

6. See Meillet, "Quelques hypothèses sur des interdictions de vocabulaire dans les langues indo-européennes", *Linguistique historique et linguistique générale,* I (Paris, 1906), 281.

7. See Meillet, *MSL,* XIV, 478.

8. The importance of this form has been acknowledged independently by both H. Pedersen and the present writer. See *BSL,* XII, lxxxv (séance du 7 juin 1902).

CHAPTER XVIII

1. See Blankenstein, *IF,* XXI, 100.

2. R. Meister (*Berichte* of the Leipzig Academy, LVI, 18) argues the existence of a vestigial instrumental case in Cypriot and Pamphylian. However, this hypothesis rests on very fragile bases.

CHAPTER XIX

1. Other examples may be found in Ch. Neue and C. Wagener, *Formenlehre der lateinischen Sprache,* I, 3rd ed. (Leipzig, 1902), 31.

CHAPTER XX

1. See Meillet, *MSL,* XIV, 361.
2. Some of the following cognates have already been noted in Meillet, *Recherches sur l'emploi du génitif-accusatif en vieux slave* (Paris, 1897), p. 94.
3. See J. Wackernagel, *KZ,* XLI, 305.
4. See Meillet, *MSL,* XIX, 348.
5. See H. Pedersen, *Vergleichende Grammatik der keltischen Sprachen,* I (Göttingen, 1908–09), 97.
6. See E. Lidén, *IF,* XIX, 338.
7. For a detailed study, see H. Hirt, *Zeitschrift für deutsche Philologie,* XXIX, 296.
8. See A. Fick, *Vergleichendes Wörterbuch der indogermanischen Sprachen,* 4th ed. (Göttingen, 1890), II, 200.
9. See W. Stokes, *KZ,* XL, 243.
10. See H. Pedersen, op. cit. (above, note 5), p. 89.

CONCLUSION

1. See Meillet, *IF,* XXI, 347.
2. For a similar observation on the relation between the Greek and Sanskrit phenomena, see H. Oldenberg, *Zeitschrift der Deutschen morgenländischen Gesellschaft,* LXI, 814.

Index verborum

NOTE: FORMS APPEARING WHOLLY OR PRIN-
cipally in Roman transcription are listed first, followed
by those in Greek transcription. In the alphabetical order-
ing of the former, the following equivalences will be
observed: æ = ae, β = b, δ = d, ə = e, γ = g, ł = l, θ = th,
þ = th.

malaf, Wel., 52
malazn, MBret., 162
malem, Arm., 52
málti, Lith., 86
(k u-)m a l t u, Umbr., 52
malù, Lith., 52
mālum, Lat., 35
mālus, Lat., 162
mąm, Av., 43
mām, OPers., 43
mắm, Skr., 43
máma, Skr., 43
mamaddhí, Skr., 80
mamrúṣī, Skr., 133
mamṛvā́n, Skr., 133
man, Goth., 133, 134, 141
mán, Lith., 64
man, OE., 134
mana, Av., 43
manā, OPers., 43
manags, Goth., 39
manei, Lith., 64
maneō, Lat., 52
m a n f, Umbr., 162
manfar, It., 108
manim, Osc., 52, 162
manst, OE., 134
mant, Wel., 162
mánthati, Skr., 108
mánthitavaí, Ved., 86
manus, Lat., 52, 162
m a n u v e, Umbr., 52
mányate, Skr., 138
map, Bryth., 56
maqi, OgamIr., 53, 56
mard, Arm., 38, 163
mare, Lat., 39
marei, Goth., 39
mārès, Lith., 39
marǝta, Av., 38
márgas, Lith., 91
mari(-saiws), Goth., 39
mártaḥ, Skr., 38, 163

martiya, OPers., 38
mártyaḥ, Skr., 38, 163
maryā́dā, Skr., 39
mast, OHG., 162
mastr, OIce., 162
mašyō, Av., 38, 163
maṭ, Av., 43
mát, Skr., 43
matan, Ir., 162
mathnắti, Skr., 108
maximus, Lat., 55
me, Av., 43
me, Skr., 43
media, Lat., 51
medius, Lat., 14
m e f i a í, Osc., 14
m e f i ú, Osc., 51
mēg, Arm., 163
megháḥ, Skr., 163
mehe, Umbr., 49, 149
mǝhmaidī́, GAv., 45
mel̄, Lat., 158
mḗlas, Lith., 67
melim, Ir., 52
melją, OSl., 52
melo, Itn., 35
melr, Arm., 158
mélżu, Lith., 87
memaid, Ir., 134
meminī́, Lat., 134
menicc, Ir., 39
mennei, OPruss., 64
mentum, Lat., 162
mentùrè, Lith., 108
meoluc, OAS., 87
mér, OIce., 149
meṣṭa, Skr., 89
mǫsti, Sl., 86
metą, OSl., 66
mętą, OSl., 108
mētāt, Lett., 66
metati, OSl., 66
mětati, OSl., 66

Index nominum

WITHDRAWN